TOASTMASTER'S

Quips & Stories

AND HOW TO USE THEM

TOASTMASTER'S

Quips & Stories

AND HOW TO USE THEM

Herbert V. Prochnow

 Sterling Publishing Co., Inc.   New York

Library of Congress Cataloging in Publication Data

Prochnow, Herbert Victor, 1897–
  Toastmaster's quips and stories and how to use
them.

  Includes index.
  1. Wit and humor. 2. Anecdotes. 3. Quotations.
I. Title.
PN6153.P75   808.88′2   81-85040
ISBN 0-8069-0238-8   AACR2
ISBN 0-8069-0239-6 (lib. bdg.)

Contents

Preface

This book contains close to 1,500 humorous stories, epigrams and amusing definitions, illustrations of wisdom, knowledge and learning, and stories of achievement, inspiration and greatness.

A significant number of these stories and quotations are taken from unusual speeches, sermons and observations by persons who have distinguished themselves in many walks of life.

All items are indexed so that a story that illustrates happiness and success, for example, as well as wisdom, may be found quickly. These items are therefore available for use on many different occasions.

There are in this book so many items of humor, wisdom and inspiration that it is hoped almost every reader will find useful subject matter. But there are a number of special groups for whom this book will be an especially valuable reference, and they will be able to use it on many occasions. For example, it should be particularly helpful to speakers, toastmasters, teachers, ministers, lawyers, and presidents of clubs or associations.

Almost every person who has had charge of a meeting or who has made a speech has searched for a humorous story, pertinent quip, or inspiring illustration that would make the remarks more effective. It takes only a few minutes to select such helpful material from this book.

Moreover, in the wide variety of its items, ranging through humor, wisdom and inspiration, the general reader also will find the book of interest and personally useful.

Herbert V. Prochnow

1

How to Use Humorous Stories and Illustrations

To speak effectively, it is often helpful to use humorous stories or illustrations of inspiration and wisdom.

You may remember how often Lincoln used both humor and illustrations. Lincoln had been called "two-faced" by a political opponent. Lincoln replied, "I leave it to my audience: if I had another face to wear, do you think I would wear this one?" He once said of an opponent, "He can compress the most words into the smallest ideas of any man I ever met." On another occasion he gave a serious quotation, "My early life is characterized in a single line of Gray's *Elegy*: 'The short and simple annals of the poor.' "

Winston Churchill was once stopped by a woman who said, "Doesn't it thrill you, Mr. Churchill, to know that every time you make a speech the hall is packed to overflowing?"

Churchill replied, "It is quite flattering. But whenever I feel this way I always remember that, if instead of making a political speech, I was being hanged, the crowd would be twice as big."

Humor

Your humor in a speech, in conducting a meeting or in conversation may take different forms. It may be a humorous story or a humorous quip or epigram. The humor should relate closely to what you wish to say, or it may be a waste of time. However, if it is directly related to what you are discussing, it can be very effective.

There are a few rules which it is well to observe in telling humorous stories:

1. Make the story as short as possible. A long story with only a little laugh falls flat. Do not add a great deal of needless detail to a story.

2. Tell the story in your own language.

3. Avoid dialects unless you are good at them.

4. Do not keep repeating the humorous part of the story to be certain everyone understands how good it is.

5. If a story produces no smiles or laughter, do not retell it in the hope that you will do better next time. You make few friends when you slap

someone on the back and say, "Boy, wasn't that a good story I just told you!" Do not lead the laughter for your own joke.

6. A story making fun of yourself or of some mistake you made is usually well received.

7. The humorous punch line of a story should come exactly at the end and not in the middle of the story. If the punch line comes before the end, the rest of the story is an anticlimax.

8. Do not try to tell a story you do not know well. You are completely lost if you say, "I'm not certain. Let's see. I think the story goes this way. No, that's not it." Frankly, it's better to forget the whole thing than to get lost in struggling to tell the story.

9. If you can use actual names with a story, it will be even more effective.

10. Generally, it is not good to tell a humorous story dealing with a subject about which the listener is wholly uninformed. A story about cricket probably wouldn't be funny to most Americans. A humorous story about farming might bring little response from an accountant in a city office, but it might be appreciated by salesmen of farm implements.

11. Do not use humorous stories which cast some reflection on the person to whom you are talking. Never use humor to injure others. You also gain nothing by telling off-color stories, except the wrong kind of reputation.

12. The point of the story must not be apparent before you finish the story, but must come as a complete surprise. The element of surprise creates the humor.

Sometimes a humorous story or a brief humorous comment is of great help when the conversation becomes heated. It may even help in avoiding a serious argument. A discussion in which tempers flare is ordinarily bad. People say things they do not mean and that sometimes are not easily forgotten. If you find yourself in such a situation, give the conversation a light or humorous touch, if you possibly can. When the discussion resumes, it will start on a less heated level.

Representatives of two groups may be discussing a subject on which there is a fundamental difference of opinion. Bill, a member of the group, finally says, "Well, I guess you have me up a tree on that point. Don't shoot, I'll come down." There is a ripple of laughter among all of them, in which Bill joins. Even those who disagree with Bill's general viewpoint will probably say to themselves, "Bill is fair. He admits it when he is wrong." After the laughter, Bill continues, "But on the second point, the following facts seem to me unanswerable." By his fairness and his touch of humor, Bill has strengthened his position.

While we are discussing humor, we ought to consider epigrams or short, witty comments. Epigrams or witticisms are often easier to use and more helpful in one's daily conversation than longer humorous stories. They take less time than a humorous story, and they can easily slip into speeches and conversation unannounced. Thus they are doubly effective.

The following sentences are illustrations of epigrams or witticisms:

Some people not only believe everything they hear, but they also repeat it.

If you want to live to see 90, don't look for it on the speedometer.

You don't have to be a magician to turn a conversation into an argument.

The Government seems to believe there is a taxpayer born every minute.

When you know nothing but good about a person, it's more fun to talk about someone else.

Ignorance combined with silence is sometimes mistaken for wisdom.

Few things are as bad as enthusiastic ignorance.

Misfortune is a point of view. Your headache feels good to an aspirin salesman.

To speak clearly is the first test of good conversation and speech. The listener must understand the idea you are trying to convey. Everything else must give way to your effort to obtain clarity of expression. Always speak directly to the point. Humorous stories and epigrams should never befuddle, confuse, or sidetrack the objective of your conversation. Use them for emphasis and to make your conversation or speech more interesting, convincing, and impressive.

This book has hundreds of humorous stories and epigrams which may be used to make your speeches and your daily conversation colorful, sparkling, and more interesting. The ability to talk effectively and speak well is an asset of immeasurable value whether you are speaking to one person or addressing an audience of two hundred people.

Don't try to make the humorous story an effective tool in your conversation and speeches in order to become known as a teller of humorous stories. The purpose of a humorous story or quip is to help improve your conversation and speeches.

Serious Illustrations

However, stories need not always be humorous. Serious and inspiring stories of remarkable achievement and of overcoming handicaps may often be greatly helpful. Parents tell their children such inspiring stories. Biographies of distinguished men and women are filled with them.

In this book you will find many illustrations of inspiration and wisdom which will help you to use the gift of conversation and speech to your greatest advantage. Most persons find conversation or speeches more interesting if one includes an occasional pertinent comment from someone else or an illustration from the life of another person.

Finally, here are some suggestions that may help you to speak more effectively and with greater self-assurance.

1. Never agree to speak on a subject regarding which you are not qualified. Nothing takes the place of knowledge of a subject. There are a number of persons who believe being able to get up and speak without fear is the major objective in speaking. That is important, but it is far more important to say something. That takes preparation.

2. You must carefully prepare every speech. No speaker has the right to take the time of an audience if not prepared.

3. Your ideas must be logically presented so that your comments are convincing. It may be best to outline your comments, point by point.

4. It is generally best to adhere closely to the subject as you prepared it. If you digress, there is great danger you will ramble.

5. Stories, illustrations and examples which are related to your subject help to emphasize your points.

6. Enthusiasm is essential. However, enthusiasm is largely the result of knowing your subject. You cannot enthuse about what you do not know. Good preparation and knowledge also give you confidence.

7. Speak clearly and loudly enough to be heard.

8. Never underestimate the intelligence of your audience. The audience deserves the best you can give them.

9. As a rule most speakers will find it useful to divide a speech into three parts:

    A. An introduction indicating the subject you propose to discuss. You may include a short humorous story or comment related to your subject.

    B. The body of your speech. It is generally best to divide the body into two, three, or four principal points. You will use facts, figures, illustrations and stories to make your speech interesting and convincing.

    C. The conclusion should be brief and may summarize the points you have made. You may also close with an inspiring story or quotation.

2

Making Speeches

Not Clear
I hope I'm a little more lucid in my remarks today than than the politician who was addressing a group in New England. A couple of old fellows were sitting on a bench, and the one said, "What is he talking about?"

And the other one said, "He don't say." *Louis W. Menk, Chairman, Burlington Northern, Inc.*

Be Generous
I once had occasion to introduce a colleague of mine at a large political rally in central Illinois, and before making the introduction I asked him if there were any special remarks he wanted me to make.

He leaned over to me and said, "Be generous. You're not under oath." *Philip M. Crane, Congressman*

Had the Time
Adlai Stevenson was unexpectedly called on to make a speech, and he started by wondering openly if the crowd wanted to hear him. "It is like the comment Big Ben could make to the Leaning Tower of Pisa: 'I've got the time if you've got the inclination.' "

A Few Comments
At a formal dedication, Calvin Coolidge was asked to perform the conventional rites of turning over the first shovelful of dirt in the traditional ground-breaking ceremonies. He did so, and was about to toss down his shovel, when an aide hastily reminded him that it was protocol to say a few words.

Calvin looked at the newly-dug earth and said softly, "You got some nice fishing worms here," and then walked off.

The Dope
Former Senator Kenneth B. Keating tells about a letter from Rochester inviting him to speak. "I hope you can come, Senator, because all of us would like to hear the dope from Washington," it said.

Confused

Adlai Stevenson told the story about the time he spoke in Chicago, and a woman came up and said, "Oh, Mr. Stevenson, you were absolutely superfluous."

And he said, "Thank you, Madam."

And she said, "I hope you publish those remarks that you made today."

And he said, "Well, Madam, in view of what you said, perhaps I should publish them posthumously."

She said, "Do—and the sooner the better!"

Typical?

A speaker was rushed to the hospital and an inexperienced nurse was assigned to him. She put a barometer in his mouth instead of a thermometer, and it read, "Dry and windy."

Kept On Talking

Mark Twain commented that he kept on talking until he had an audience cowed.

Speech

New Jersey's former governor, Robert B. Meyner, confesses he's getting a little concerned about the reputation he has as a talker. One restaurant owner, he said, put a candid picture of him with his mouth open in a window immediately below a sign reading: "Open 24 Hours a Day."

Useless Words

If all the useless words spoken were placed end to end, they would reach some fellow who is trying his level best to concentrate. *Granite City (Illinois) Press Record*

Saying Nothing

Most of us know how to say nothing—few of us know when.

Variations on the Old Line

Leopold Fechtner, who collects humor, says he seldom hears anything new from comedians. "At most, I get variations of the original. Once I listed all the variations the comics were telling about the old line—'Old soldiers never die, they just fade away.' This is what I got: 'Old pickpockets never die, they just steal away.' 'Old fishermen never die, they just smell that way.' 'Old photographers never die, they just stop developing.' 'Old accountants never die, they just lose their balance.' 'Old travellers never die, they just lose their grip.' 'Old actors never die, they just act that way.' 'Old lawyers never die, they just lose their appeal.' 'Old fatties never diet, they just eat away.' " *Modern Maturity*

Definition
After-dinner speaker: The gust of honor.

Platitude
She plunged into a sea of platitudes and with the powerful breast stroke of a channel swimmer made her confident way towards the white cliffs of the obvious. *W. Somerset Maugham*

Oratory
Oratory is the art of making deep sounds from the chest seem like important messages from the brain.

News Headline
"Farmers Hear Pest Talk"—We've heard him also.

Subtlety
The art of saying what you think and getting out of range before it is understood.

It Isn't Easy
Whenever I am asked to speak, all thoughts desert my head. My knocking knees grow water-weak and I perspire with dread. "As unaccustomed as I am . . ." was truly meant for me, and I will shun whene'er I can the speaker's misery. Oh many a time and oft have I turned red and green and blue, when someone poked me in the ribs and hissed "It's time for you!" I'd rather track a hungry lion and beard him in his den, than rise and face at half-past nine a bunch of well-fed men! *Optimist Magazine*

A Short Speech
Airplane pioneers Orville and Wilbur Wright were more than taciturn. Above all, they hated to make speeches and avoided them, whenever possible. One day at a luncheon attended by a number of inventors, Wilbur was called on by the toastmaster.

"There must be some mistake," stammered Wilbur. "Orville is the one who does the talking."

The toastmaster turned to him.

Orville stood up and announced, "Wilbur just made the speech."

The Same Thing?
Once upon a time a young man attempted to write an advertisement to describe a new kind of soap. Here is what he produced:

"The alkaline element and fats in this product are blended in such a way as to secure the highest quality of saponification, along with a specific gravity that keeps it on top of the water, relieving the bather of the trouble and annoyance of fishing around for it at the bottom of the tub during his ablutions.''

A more experienced writer later wrote the same thing in two words: ''It floats.''

Good Speeches
No speech can be entirely bad if it's short enough. *Irvin S. Cobb*

Brevity
The story of creation is told in Genesis in 400 words; the Ten Commandments contain only 297 words; Lincoln's Gettysburg Address is but 266 words in length; and the Declaration of Independence required but 1,321 words to set up a new concept of freedom.

A Good Beginning
Author Ian MacLaren once counselled a group of budding writers: ''Begin your story well—it's half the battle. Always bear in mind the case of the young man, who, desiring to marry, obtained a favorable hearing from his sweetheart's father by opening the interview with the words: 'I know a way, sir, whereby you can save a lot of money.' ''

Bad Speeches
Speak when you are angry, and you will make the finest speech you will ever regret.

Argument
No one ever won an argument that lost a friend.

Toastmaster
The toastmaster is the person who rises after the dinner and tells you the best part of the evening is over.

Heard the Joke
The man we like in the audience is Jasper Penn; he's heard the joke, but he laughs again.

Rhetorical Question
When a person says he can't make a speech, why doesn't he stop?

Baseball
The teacher directed the class to write a brief account of a baseball game. All the pupils were busy except one boy who wrote never a word. The teacher gave him an additional five minutes. The fifth minute had almost elapsed when the boy scrawled a sentence: ''Rain—no game.''

Boner

"As I look over the audience I see many faces I should like to shake hands with."

Clear and Concise

"Shut up," he said, for he had been taught at Harvard to speak concisely.

Some Speakers

You have to listen for a long time to find out that some speakers have nothing to say.

Be Careful How You Speak

Any ordinary sentence can be made to have as many meanings as it can have variations of inflection. For example: If we were to say, "I never said he stole money," what would it mean? It's all in the way we say it. There are six words in the sentence; by emphasizing each word separately, we get six different meanings. Read them aloud, and see:

I never said he stole money.
I *never* said he stole money.
I never *said* he stole money.
I never said *he* stole money.
I never said he *stole* money.
I never said he stole *money*.

A Famous Toast to Water

William Jennings Bryan gave his brilliant toast to water, after refusing wine at a dinner given in his honor in Japan:

"A daily need for every living thing. It rises from the earth obedient to the summons of the sun, and descends in showers of blessings. It gives of its beauty to the fragrant flowers; it is the alchemy that transmutes base clay to golden grain. It is the canvas on which the finger of the Infinite traces the radiant bow of promise. It is the drink that cheers, and brings no sorrow. Jehovah, upon Creation's dawn, said, 'It is good.'"

3

Business As Usual

That's Different
A contractor wanted to give a government official a sports car.

The official objected saying, "Sir, common decency and my basic sense of honor would never permit me to accept a gift like that."

The contractor said, "I quite understand. Suppose we do this. I'll sell you the sports car for $10."

The official thought a moment. "In that case, I'll take two."

Computers
We suppose when these machines with brains finally take over the world, they'll make as many improvements in us as we made in them.

That Will Take Care of Him
"Thirty dollars to paint my garage? That's outrageous! I wouldn't pay Michelangelo that much to paint my garage!"

"Listen, you," said the painter, "if he does the job for any less, we'll come and picket your place!"

Careers
Some people chisel out a career—others just chisel.

Definitions
Business: What, when you haven't got any, you go out of.

Night watchman: A man who earns his living without doing a day's work.

Hard job: One which leaves you as tired before the weekend as after.

Really Short
POLICEMAN: Can you describe your missing cashier?
BUSINESSMAN: He is about five feet five inches tall and $7,000 short.

Common Ailment
Most people's financial problems are simple. They're short of money.

When Money Talks

When money talks, few people are hard of hearing.

When money talks, no one pays attention to the grammar.

How True . . .

A million dollars doesn't always bring happiness. A man with ten million dollars is no happier than a man with nine million dollars.

A Great Fortune

It takes a great deal of boldness mixed with a vast amount of caution, to acquire a great fortune; but then it takes ten times as much wit to keep it after you have got it as it took to make it. *Mayer A. Rothschild*

The Money Market

You can buy a Russian ruble cheap, but no one with cents would do it.

Currency

Dollar bill: A form of currency that ought to have on it a homing pigeon instead of an eagle.

A $2 bill is not only unlucky, but it won't buy anything either.

Send Him

There is a story, made up, that the American Embassy in India advertised for volunteers to go to the moon. Three volunteers came forward.

One was from the North, a Sikh, a bearded, turbaned gentleman. He said, "I'll go to the moon if you give me one million dollars."

Another gentleman, from the center of India, said, "I'll go if you give me two million dollars."

And the third gentleman, who belonged to the business community said, "I'll go if you give me three million dollars."

So the American Embassy representative asked them, "First, if I give you one million dollars, what will you do with it?"

The first said, "I'll burn it up, enjoy life, and then I don't mind going anywhere."

The second man said, "I want two million dollars. One million I'll spend in enjoying life, and the second million I will give to my family. I don't mind taking the trip."

The third man said, "I want three million. One million to enjoy life. The second million for my family. And the third million I'll give to the Sikh to send him up to the moon." *Triloki Nath Kaul, Ambassador from India to the U.S.*

Definition

Banking is a business in which you maintain liquidity to achieve solidity.

Be More Careful

The new bank president was being introduced to the employees.

He singled out one of the men at the tellers' windows, questioning him in detail about his work.

"I have been here 40 years," said the teller, with conscious pride, "and in all that time I only made one slight mistake."

"Good," replied the president. "Let me congratulate you. But hereafter be more careful."

Typical Banker

A small town bank gained the title to a filling station via a foreclosure. To demonstrate his concern that the newly acquired enterprise was being run efficiently, the bank president sent one of his loan officers to the gas station to check the operation.

The loan officer decided to get the feel of the business by helping out at the pumps. When his first customer said, "Fill 'er up," the banker started to spring into action, but then asked the customer:

"How far are you going?"

"Just down to the state line," the customer replied.

"Then you won't need a full tank," cautioned the banker. "I'll let you have five gallons."

Easy to Save

It's easy to save if you can make money faster than the family can spend it.

Foolish

A banker declares it's foolish to keep money around the house. It's not only foolish, but impossible.

A Little Difficult

The employees of a bank went on strike, leaving teller functions to the bank officers. A customer phoned the bank during the strike and asked if the bank was open.

"Yes," she was told, "we have two windows open."

After much hesitation, the customer meekly asked, "You mean I can't come in through the front door?"

Definition

Credit is the system whereby a person who can't pay gets another person who can't pay to guarantee that he can pay. *Charles Dickens*

Half the World

One half the world knows how the other half lives, but they don't know how many installments they're behind.

Everything on Credit

You can get about everything on credit now except some good easy money.

You can't tell how much a man still owes on his car by how high he holds his chin.

Debts

After you contract a debt, it seems to expand.

Debtor and Creditor

A debtor is a man who owes money. A creditor is one who thinks he's going to get it.

Going Broke

WILLIE: Would you loan me a dollar, Charlie?
CHARLIE: Sure!
WILLIE: Thanks. Just give me fifty cents.
CHARLIE: Okay with me, old man. Here it is.
WILLIE: Now you still owe me fifty cents, don't you?
CHARLIE: Sure thing.
WILLIE: And I owe you fifty cents, so that makes us square again. Good-bye!

The Sad Truth

We like the man who says yes better than the one who says no, but the trouble is the former seldom has any money to lend.

Never call a man stupid before you see whether he would lend you $20.

Committees

The morning after Charles Lindbergh flew the Atlantic an associate rushed into Charles Kettering's laboratory in Dayton, Ohio, shouting: "He made it! Lindbergh landed safely in Paris!" Kettering went on working. The associate spoke again: "Think of it—Lindbergh flew the Atlantic alone! He did it all by himself!"

Kettering looked up from his work and remarked quietly: "Certainly—when he flies it with a committee, let me know." *R. S. Reynolds, Jr.*

Committee: The unready, who have been appointed by the unwilling, to do the unnecessary.

Sometimes a business is so busy that the officers don't have time for long committee meetings.

Conferences

A conference is a gathering of important people who singly can do nothing, but together can decide that nothing can be done. *Fred Allen*

A business conference is a meeting where you discuss something at length without making a decision.

Confidential

A confidential memorandum in business deals with something everybody knows, but it's typewritten instead of mimeographed.

Carbon Copies

In business, carbon copies are what you make to fill files, so clerks can be employed keeping track of records they can't find.

Competition

Competition is a battle in which incompetence dies.

A New Product

The development of a new product is a three-step process: First, an American firm announces an invention; second, the Russians claim they made the same discovery twenty years ago; third, the Japanese start exporting it.

Great Invention

The computer is a great invention. There are just as many mistakes as ever, but they are nobody's fault.

In and Out of the Office

The businessman who demands facts in his office buys hair restorer from a bald-headed barber.

Apology Accepted

I'm a self-made man.
I accept your apology.

Lucky

An executive came home and slumped in his favorite chair with a discouraged look. His wife asked what was wrong.

"You know these aptitude tests we're giving at the office? Well, I took one today and it's a good thing I own the company!"

Cheap

SMART ALEC: How much are your fifty dollar shoes?
ALERT CLERK: Twenty-five dollars a foot.

Salesmanship

Sign in a store window: "Don't go elsewhere to be cheated. Come in here."

A man without a smiling face must not open a shop. *Chinese Proverb*

That Fixed Him

During the meat shortage, a butcher placed his last chicken on the scale. "That'll be $2.95," he told the customer.

"That one's too small; don't you have anything larger?" the woman asked.

The canny butcher returned the chicken to the refrigerator, paused a moment, then took it out again. "This one," he announced, "will be $3.60."

"Fine," the customer smiled. "I'll take them both."

Economics

Only one fellow in ten thousand understands the currency question, and we meet him every day. *Kin Hubbard*

Not Worried

One businessman to another: "Recessions don't bother me. I went bankrupt once during a boom."

New Era

With a business boom, some economists aren't sure whether it is a new era or the day before the morning after.

Smart Lad

An American history teacher, lecturing the class on Puritan fables and foibles asked: "What sort of people were punished in the stocks?" To which a small voice from the back of the room responded: "The small investor."

Take a Ride on the Reading

In an updated Monopoly game, the player who buys all four railroads goes bankrupt.

Definitions

Economics simplified: When buyers do not fall for prices, prices must fall for buyers.

An economist is a person who can explain clearly what he does not understand.

An economist is a man who knows a great deal about very little, and who goes along knowing more and more about less and less, until finally he knows practically everything about nothing.

An economist is a person who knows exactly what is going to happen, except he is not quite sure.

Stable economy: What you had in the horse-and-buggy days.

Progress?

The farmer raised two chickens and sold them to a city man and with the proceeds bought two shirts. The city man now had two chickens and the farmer two shirts.

A planner advised the farmer to shorten up on supply so as to increase the price. Accordingly the farmer raised but one chicken and took it to the market, selling it for the price of two—but when he bought a shirt it cost him twice as much as formerly. The city man had one chicken and the farmer one shirt.

Backward Nations

An economist says the people of backward nations must be jacked up to higher economic levels. Well, jack is what it takes.

Looking Forward

The person who works and saves will someday have enough to divide with those who don't.

Reform

Necessity reforms the poor, and satiety reforms the rich. *Tacitus*

Is That Clear?

"We must change the status quo around here!" proclaimed the speaker loudly.

"What's the status quo?" whispered a woman to her husband beside her.

"That's Latin for the mess we're in," he explained.

Something for Nothing

It is unfortunate that so many citizens in this country are demanding something for nothing. It is even more unfortunate that they are getting it.

What Is an American?

An American is a fellow wearing English tweeds, a Hong Kong shirt and Spanish shoes, who sips Brazilian coffee sweetened with Philippine sugar, from a Bavarian cup while nibbling on Swiss cheese, sitting at a Danish desk over a Persian rug, after coming home in a German car from an Italian movie . . . and writes his congressman with a Japanese ballpoint pen on French paper, demanding that he do something about foreigners taking away our foreign markets.

Good News?

WIFE: I have some good news for you.

HUSBAND: What?

WIFE: You haven't been paying those auto insurance premiums for nothing!

Makes a Difference

Overheard on the beach: "Mummy, may I go in for a swim?"

"Certainly not, my dear, it's far too deep."

"But Daddy is swimming."

"Yes, dear, but he is insured."

Made No Difference

Two sweet little old ladies came to the ticket counter, purchased their tickets, checked their bags, and were on their way to the boarding area when they passed the insurance concession. "Aren't you going to buy some insurance?" the one asked the other. "No," replied sweet little old lady number one, "I always used to, but it never seemed to make any difference." *John H. Shaffer*

How He Started

Fountain pen manufacturer Lewis E. Waterman began his business career as an insurance agent. At one time, after working on a client for several weeks, he persuaded the man to take out a large policy.

Waterman called on him with the contract ready for signature. He placed it on the desk and took a fountain pen from his pocket. As he opened it, it began to leak and ink ran over the contract.

Waterman hurried back to his office for another policy form. By the time he returned, however, the man had changed his mind. Waterman was so disgusted that he gave up the insurance business and devoted his time to the development of a reliable fountain pen. *E. E. Edgar, Omaha World-Herald*

Not Feeling So Well

A constituent of mine found himself in court, all bandaged up, with a cast on one leg and a cast on an arm, and his head bandaged. It was an obvious insurance case.

The judge knew him and leaned over and said, "George, how do you feel?" George said, "Judge, I don't think I'm going to make it. I think I'm going to die."

The judge said, "I don't understand that. I have the accident report here from the police. Trooper McIntyre asked how you felt after the accident, and you said you felt fine."

"Judge, you haven't got it right," he said. "I was going home from my neighbor's farm on my own rig, and just as I was about to turn in the gate, a big trailer jackknifed and knocked me into the ditch. When I came to, there was McIntyre's blue light going round and round. He walked down to where my mule was in the ditch, shook his head, pulled out his gun and shot her. Then he came over with his gun smoking, looked down at me and said, 'How do you feel?' I said, 'I feel fine.' " *Secretary of the Interior Rogers C. B. Morton, as told to the Executives Club of Chicago*

Saves Insurance Costs

SMITH: Why is your car painted blue on one side, and red on the other side?

JONES: It's a great scheme. You should hear the witnesses contradicting each other.

Life Insurance & Taxes

Taxes and life insurance are just about the same thing. You pay out the money, and someone else has the fun of spending it.

First True Life Insurance Policy

When William Gibbons of London, in the year 1583, became the first man in history to take out a true life insurance policy, he paid a one-year premium of eight pounds sterling for a death benefit of 100 pounds.

The transaction was made possible for two reasons: The insurors were willing to bet 12½-to-1 that William would last out the year, while William was willing to pay this outrageous premium in the confidence that if the grim reaper should catch up to him within that time the 100 pounds for his family would have substantial value.

It is the confidence in the future of money that is the rock on which the insurance business is based. *Jenkin Lloyd Jones*

Wait Until You See Me

I know a young boy down in New York in one of the suburbs. He's fourteen years of age. When the summer vacation came along he decided to get a job and earn some money.

He looked in the want ads and there was one: "Wanted: A bright boy age fourteen; show up tomorrow at eight o'clock," and it gave an address.

The next morning he was there not at eight, but at ten minutes of eight, only to find there were twenty bright young boys, age fourte, waiting in line for the job. He walked in, saw the twenty boys, and knew that anyone of them could qualify and get the job ahead of him. He was now the twenty-first kid in line.

The situation was inauspicious.

The average boy would have said, "Well, I tried; I got down here. What can I do? Any one of these kids looks bright, and they're the right age, and one of them will get the job."

But this boy was made of sterner stuff. He realized that he had a problem, so he went at the problem by the process of thought, and thought will always produce an idea.

He took a piece of paper and he wrote something on it. He walked over to the secretary of the man doing the hiring. He bowed low to her, politely, and he said, "It is very vital that you deliver this important message to your boss immediately."

She was so impressed with him that she took the note. She examined it and smiled. She said, "Yes, sir." She immediately went into the inner office; laid the note down in front of her boss. He read it and laughed out loud.

This is what it said:

"Dear Sir: I am the twenty-first kid in line. Don't do anything until you see me."

Did he, or did he not get the job? *Norman Vincent Peale*

Just Barks

The sportsman went to a hunting lodge and bagged a record number of birds with the help of a dog named "Salesman."

The following year, the man wrote the lodge again for reservations, requesting the same dog, "Salesman."

As soon as he arrived at the lodge, he asked the handler if "Salesman" was to hunt.

"Hound ain't no good now," the handler said.

"What happened?" said the man. "Was he injured?"

"Nope! Some fool came down here and called him 'Sales Manager' all week. Now all he does is sit on his tail and bark."

Extras

The farmer in the midwest had been taken in so many times by the local car dealer that when the dealer wanted to buy a cow, the farmer priced it to him like this: Basic cow, $400; Two-tone extra, $90; Extra stomach, $150; Produce storage compartment, $120; Dispensing device: Four spigots at $20 each, $80; Genuine cowhide upholstery, $250; Dual horns, $30; Automatic fly swatter, $70; Total $1,095.

They Never Do

The applicant for a sales job stood before the sales manager. "Your references, please."

The lad smiled. "I didn't bring any. Like my picture, they don't do me justice."

The Best Kind

At a village store in the Blue Ridge country the old proprietor was trying to sell a wastebasket to a hillbilly. Sales resistance was strong. "How come I need a basket? It'll need emptyin' every month or so."

"Not this one," said the proprietor. "Ain't got no bottom to it. Just move it a jot."

Influencing People

Benjamin Franklin was an accomplished salesman. Seeking to win the friendship of a man who had attacked him in a speech, Franklin wrote him a note of appreciation; they became lifelong friends.

LaSalle, the noted French explorer, gained the goodwill of hostile Indians by addressing them in their own language and using their style of oratory.

Emil Ludwig said of Napoleon in the Italian campaign: "Half of what he achieves is achieved by the power of words." Sometimes the general told his ragged, hungry army about the good food and comfortable lodging they would find beyond the mountains; on other occasions he pictured his soldiers returning as heroes to their home towns.

Reminding Him

A salesman always kept his hat on while doing "desk work" at the office. When kidded about it, he answered, "That's to remind me I really ought not to be there!"

A Salesman with Imagination

It was an imaginative experiment by a desperate American tea salesman that gave us one of our favorite summer beverages, iced tea. Tea had been drunk hot through all the ages it has been known, until 1904, at the St. Louis World's Fair. A salesman named Richard Blechnyden, we are told, came to the Fair to promote Indian and Ceylon teas. But the weather was miserably hot, and iced drink stands were doing all the business. Who wanted hot tea? So he decided to make his tea into an iced drink, too. He made it stronger than usual, to make up for the melting ice he put into it. It tasted good to him, and so it did to everyone else. Iced tea was an instant success. It still is, so much that we drink an estimated twelve billion glasses a year. The next time you enjoy a cool glass of iced tea, remember that ingenious salesman.

Industry

This is a year when we need emphasis on the try in industry.

Maxims of Business

These six rules were found in a businessman's Bible published in the 1800's. They were read at a prayer meeting of the Christian Business Men's Committee of Triple Cities, New York.

1. Engage in no business inconsistent with the strictest morality, nor in which you cannot daily seek the blessing of the Most High.

2. Follow your chosen vocation, and that alone, whatever temptations to speculation or rapid acquisition may present themselves.

3. Adopt no "tricks of trade," however sanctioned by custom, that involve deception or untruthfulness.

4. Never incur a debt beyond your resources.

5. Always live within your income.

6. Devote a fixed portion of your income, beforehand, to charitable uses, to be employed and accounted for as systematically as family expenditures. The man who will regulate his business by such simple rules as these may free himself from the feverish excitements of adventurous traffickers, and secure himself, with God's blessing, of an honest competency, if not a benevolent affluence, and a good name. *Praying Hands*

A Businessman's Prayer

Help me, O Lord, to remember that three feet make one yard, sixteen ounces one pound, four quarts one gallon, and sixty minutes one hour. Help me to do business on the square. Make me sympathetic with the fellow who has broken in the struggle. Keep me from taking an unfair advantage of the weak, or from selling my self-respect for a profit. Blind my eyes to the petty faults of others, but reveal to me my own. And when comes the sound of low music, the scent of sweet flowers, and the crunch of footsteps on the gravel, make the ceremony short, and the epitaph simply—"Here lies a man . . . one who was of service to others." *Evans Echoes*

4

One-Upmanship

Relieved

Jack Benny liked to tell about the time he carried his violin case to the White House to play for the President.

A guard stopped him at the door and asked: "What's in the case?"

Thinking he was being funny, Benny replied, "Just a machine gun."

"Thank heavens!" deadpanned the guard. "I was afraid it might be your violin."

Evidence

"Will the person who took the cake from the sergeant's desk at police headquarters kindly return same. It is needed as evidence in a food poisoning case." *The Drive Wheel, Newton, Kansas*

Getting Even

A doctor was awakened at 4 a.m. to make a house call. He reluctantly got dressed and braved a snowstorm. After the examination, he told his patient to send immediately for his lawyer and relatives and friends and make a will.

The doctor got home and told his wife what he had done.

His wife asked, "Was he that bad?"

The doctor said, "No, but I just didn't want to be the only sucker called out on a night like this."

Perfect Fit

A young, newly-married minister who was living on a meager salary became very upset one day when his wife came home with an expensive new dress. He chided her for the purchase, saying, "You know that we can't afford something like this."

She said, "I know. I shouldn't have purchased it, but the Devil tempted me." And he said to her, "Why didn't you say, 'Get thee behind me, Satan'!"

She said, "I did, and then he whispered over my shoulder in my ear, 'It fits you just beautifully in back, too'." *Donald J. Griffin*

30

Too Many Against Us

My present difficulty is perhaps illustrated by the story of George Bernard Shaw attending the opening of one of his early plays. After the final curtain, in response to the cries of "Author!" "Author!" he went to the stage amid a tremendous ovation. When the audience became silent, a loud, eloquent, and profound, "Boo! Boo! Boo!" was heard from one man up in the balcony. When quiet was restored, Shaw looked up at the balcony and said, "Sir, you up there in the balcony. I agree with you. But who are we two against so many?" *William Benton, former U.S. Senator*

Still Earlier

A rabbi was seated beside a pompous woman at a banquet.

"One of my ancestors," boasted the lady, "signed the Declaration of Independence."

"Is that so?" said the rabbi. "One of mine wrote the Ten Commandments."

We All Do

"We love our new picture window," Mrs. Jones told a visitor, "because it brings the great outdoors right into our living room."

"We get the same results cheaper," replied her guest, "with our teenager's muddy shoes."

Second Thought

A saintly-looking old fellow was running to catch his bus. Just as he appeared to be winning the race, the bus driver, with a fiendish smirk, pulled away from the curb, and the wheels splashed a shower of muddy water over the old man.

Softly, this kindly one murmured, "May his soul find peace." Still more softly he added, "And the sooner the better."

Not So Dumb

Two counterfeiters with a talented but stupid engraver found themselves with a large quantity of almost perfect bills. The trouble was, they were all $18 bills. The crooks decided to go back into the hill country to dispose of the bills, because "nobody up there sees much money." Deep in the mountains, they flashed one on a crossroads storekeeper and talked him into changing it.

"How do you want it?" he asked. "Would two sevens and a four be all right?"

Is That Clear?

Winston Churchill told about a man who waited one bitter cold night for a London-bound train. Due to some emergency, a non-stop express train halted briefly and the man climbed aboard.

"You can't get on," yelled the conductor. "This train doesn't stop here."

"Very well," replied the man calmly. "If it doesn't stop here, I'm not on it."

Take Two

Nathan Rothschild, founder of the English house of Rothschild, was made a baron by the Austrian Emperor.

He never used the title and was so unimpressed by any title that when a celebrated royal visitor was ushered into his office, Nathan offered him a chair—and went on with his work.

"I'm afraid," his visitor said haughtily, "that you did not hear me announced. I am the Prince of Puckler-Muskau."

"Ah, then," responded Nathan, looking up momentarily, "take two chairs."

Save the King

When a member of the faculty of a London medical college was appointed honorary physician to the King, he proudly wrote a notice on the blackboard in his classroom.

"Professor Jenks informs his students that he has been appointed honorary physician to His Majesty, the King."

When the Professor returned to his classroom in the afternoon, he found written below his notice, this line: "God save the King!" *Jim Hewitt*

Modest

He said he was a modest and tolerant person. He said he always listened to others present their stupid opinions.

Smart and Smarter

SMART SON: Dad, I just siphoned a couple of gallons of gas out of your car for my old bus. It's okay, isn't it?

SMARTER FATHER: Sure, it's okay, son. I bought that gas with your allowance for next week. So run along and have a good time.

Texas and Alaska

A man from Texas met a man from Alaska, and neither of them could resist the urge to play one-upmanship about the merits of their respective states.

The Texan finally conceded the Alaskan's point that Alaska was number one in terms of sheer size, but he said, "I'll bet your half-frozen citizens would love to have some of the fine, well-bred expensive cattle that we have in Texas."

"Okay," said the Alaskan, "so you have a few head of mangy cattle. But you've got nothing like our tall snow-clad mountains."

32

"Not now," shot back the Texan. "We did have, but the cattle trampled them down."

He Lost

Senator John G. Tower reports that a Texan and an Alaskan were debating the size and importance of their states on a journey by steamer along the Alaskan coast. The Texan was yielding no ground, insisting that the Lone Star State conceded first place in nothing—size, scenery, products or advantages.

As they debated, an iceberg loomed ahead. The Texan stopped, studied it a moment, then conceded, "Well, I've got to admit you've got bigger ice cubes."

Good Morning, Colonel

A young man had just finished his tour of duty and had entered the fall semester of a western university. One morning he was about ten minutes late to his class and the professor bawled him out in front of the class.

"When you were in the Air Force and came in late like this," said the professor, "what did they say to you?"

"Well, when I came in late," answered the young man, "they just said, 'How are you this morning, Colonel, sir?' and stood up and saluted!"

Imagination

A woman said to her minister, "This morning I stood in front of the mirror for half an hour admiring my beauty. Do you think I committed the sin of pride?"

The minister replied, "No, I don't think you committed the sin of pride— it was more the sin of faulty imagination."

Q & A

During a question-and-answer period one night a student asked, "Bishop Sheen, suppose you tell us how Jonah managed to survive four days in the belly of a whale."

Bishop Sheen said, "Frankly, I don't know; but when I get to Heaven I'll ask Jonah."

"Well," the youth said, "suppose Jonah didn't go to Heaven?"

"Well," Bishop Sheen said, "then you ask him!" *Grant C. Butler*

Squel-l-lch!

A rather conceited man was invited to dinner by a young lady of his acquaintance, but he did not accept.

A few days later, seeing her on the street, he said in his best manner: "I believe you asked me to dine with you last week."

The lady looked at him thoughtfully and answered: "And did you?"

Too True

The man tried to talk a traffic cop out of giving him a ticket for speeding, but to no avail.

"What do you do," he asked sarcastically, "when you find someone who is really guilty?"

"I couldn't say," the cop answered. "All I ever catch are the innocent ones!"

Was That Nice?

In a crowded theater, a young man was just about to sit down in one of a pair of empty seats when he was abruptly pushed off balance by a woman trailing behind him with her husband. Before he could recover, the couple had plumped into the seats.

"Sorry, my friend," said the husband, "we beat you!"

"That's quite all right," replied the young man. "I hope you and your mother enjoy the show."

Keeping Up

Business tycoons Joe and Dick spent their spare time trying to outdo each other. If one bought a $150 suit, the other bought one for $200. If one bought a Cadillac, the other bought a Rolls Royce.

One day Joe had a phone installed in his car. Dick immediately had one put in his car. Then he called Joe and said casually, "This is Dick. I'm phoning your car from my car."

"Would you mind holding on a minute," answered Joe. "I've got a call on another line."

First Class

A vacationer reports that while he was having a bit of lunch at a roadside restaurant, a well-dressed gentleman came in and ordered a cup of coffee. The waitress served it in a thick, heavy cup.

"Where is the saucer?" asked the man.

"We don't use saucers here," said the waitress haughtily. "The trade we serve drink out of cups."

Don't Say That Again

DEPARTING GUEST: You've got a pretty place here, Frank, but it looks a bit bare yet.

HOST: Oh, it's because the trees are rather young. I hope they'll have grown to a good size before you come again.

Forgiving

It's a great deal easier to forgive an enemy after you get even with him—or a little ahead.

Remember?

Two successful, self-made businessmen, who hadn't seen each other since their poverty-stricken childhood, met at a party. One of the men smugly began to remind the other about his humble origin.

"Remember when you only had one pair of shoes to your name, Harry?" he asked.

"I sure do," the second man replied slowly. "You asked me what they were used for."

They Got Him

Two young men, Jack and Charlie, had gone through high school and college together. Both had good jobs. One morning, Jack called Charlie and said, "They've got me."

"Who's got you?"

"The draft board. But I am going to fool them. I once had a hernia, and I am going to wear my truss."

So Jack, wearing his truss, went down to the draft board. Three doctors examined him, took out his draft card and put down "M.E." Jack said, "What's that?" They said, "Medically Exempt."

Four weeks later bright and early in the morning, Charlie called Jack and said, "They've got me."

"Who's got you?"

"The draft board."

"Haven't you something wrong—flat feet, bad back, ulcers?"

"No, I am in perfect health, as you know."

"Well then, I'll lend you my truss and you go down and make the usual complaints that you can't lift things, you have intermittent pains, and they will let you off for having a hernia."

Charlie went to the draft board. The same three doctors examined him and then took out his draft card and put down "M.E." "Medically Exempt?" asked Charlie. "No," replied the doctor. "Middle East. Anyone who can wear a truss upside down can certainly ride a camel!" *Dr. Alfred M. Lilienthal*

Blockhead

The recruit complained to the sergeant that he had a splinter in his finger.

"You should have more sense," was the harsh comment, "than to scratch your head."

Reply to a Heckler

"Don't you wish you were a man?" shouted a man in the crowd.

"No!" she shouted back. "Do you?"

Who Am I?

Of all the pestiferous persons, the one who grasps your hand and says,

"You don't know me, do you?" is the worst. Often he adds, "Now who is it? Tell me, who am I?"

Such a person one time assaulted William Howard Taft as he stood talking with a friend in Washington. The person ran up, saying, "How do you do, Mr. Taft; I bet you don't know me." Taft replied, "You win," and turned his broad back and walked away.

Hard to Explain

"Why do you weep over the sorrows of people in whom you have no interest when you go to the theatre?" asked the man.

"I don't know," replied the woman. "Why do you cheer wildly when a man with whom you are not acquainted slides safely into second base?"

How to Tell

"This is an ideal spot for a picnic."

"Yes, it must be. Fifty million insects can't be wrong."

Tit for Tat

"When George Washington was your age, son, he was a surveyor."

"And when he was your age, Dad, he was President."

Another One

A man in the insane asylum sat fishing over a flower bed. A visitor approached, and wishing to be affable, asked, "How many have you caught?" "You're the ninth," was the reply.

Prophecy

Voltaire said that in 100 years the Bible would be a forgotten book, found only in the museums. When the 100 years were up, Voltaire's home was occupied by the Geneva Bible Society.

5

Is Anyone Else Up There?

Florida State Senator Richard Pettigrew cited the difficulty of knowing just whom to trust among all those offering answers to the nagging problems faced by state legislators. It reminded him of the man who fell off the cliff, managed to grab hold of a branch on the way down, and hung there in mid-air. After yelling for quite a while, he heard a deep voice calling down to him, "I will help you."

The man admitted he was certainly ready for help, and the voice went on, "I am the Lord. Trust me. Just let go of that limb." The hanging man thought a few minutes, and then called out, "Is anyone else up there?" *From a column by Alan L. Otten in the Wall Street Journal*

Engines or Bishops?

An 86-year-old lady was on her first airplane flight. At an altitude of 28,000 feet, the following announcement came over the intercom: "This is your Captain speaking. Our number four engine has just been shut off because of mechanical trouble. However, I assure you that there is nothing to worry about. We will continue our flight with three engines and will land in Chicago on schedule . . . Also, I have some good news to assure you. We have four Methodist bishops on board."

The lady, who had listened apprehensively to every word, called the stewardess and said, "Would you please tell the Captain that I would rather have four engines and three bishops." *Told by Norman Vincent Peale in his response to the award given him at the National Bible Week Luncheon in New York. The Presbyterian Layman*

Prayer

In the days of the Civil War, a personal friend of Abraham Lincoln was a visitor at the White House. "I had been spending three weeks with Mr. Lincoln as his guest. One night—it was just after the battle of Bull Run—I was restless and could not sleep . . . from the private room where the president slept, I heard low tones, for the door was partly open. Instinctively I wandered in, and there I saw a sight which I have never forgotten. It was the president, kneeling before an open Bible . . . his back toward me. I shall never forget his prayer: 'Oh, thou God, that heard Solomon in the night when he prayed and cried for wisdom, hear me. I cannot lead these people, I cannot guide the affairs of this nation without Thy help . . . O God, hear me and save this nation.' "

George Washington, first president of the U.S., who prayed in the snow at Valley Forge, said, "The event is in the hands of God." When the tide of battle was unfavorable, Washington said, "How will it end? God will direct."

When the leaders of the United States assembled to write the constitution, it was proposed by Benjamin Franklin that each session be opened with prayer. Franklin said, "I have lived a long time, and the longer I live the more convincing proof I see of this truth—that God governs the affairs of men. And if a sparrow cannot fall to the ground without His notice, is it possible that an empire can rise without His aid?"

Maybe, Even Oftener

In our present confusion all the world needs is to cheer up and get on its toes. Of course, it might also help if it got on its knees occasionally.

Less Thunder, More Lightning

A noted clergyman was asked by a colleague why the loud, vehement preaching of his earlier days had given way to a more quiet, persuasive manner of speech. The preacher laughed. "When I was young," he said, "I thought it was the thunder that killed people, but when I grew up I discovered it was the lightning. So I determined that in the future I would thunder less and lighten more."

Same Problem

It was the start of a holiday weekend and the service station was crowded.

Finally, an attendant hustled up to the local minister, who had been waiting in line for some time.

"I'm sorry about the delay, pastor," the attendant apologized. "Seems like everybody waits until the last minute to get ready for a trip which they knew they're going on."

The pastor smiled.

"I know what you mean," he said. "I have the same problem in my business."

Bad Question

PREACHER: God created man out of mud and set him against the fence to dry.

DEACON: Does it say that?

PREACHER: Yes, the Good Book says that.

DEACON: Who built the fence?

PREACHER: Those are the kind of questions that undermine religion.

A Mistake

The Administration official was conducting two out-of-town friends on a tour of the famous Franciscan Monastery in Washington. At the information desk, an elderly friar was handing out pamphlets filled with facts about the monastery.

One visitor looked in the pamphlet and read that all the friars and brothers rise at 4 a.m., seven days a week. He went back to the old friar and said, "Surely this is a mistake."

The friar read the sentence, smiled and said, "It certainly is a mistake. But, unfortunately, it's true." *Don Maclean, Scripps-Howard Newspapers*

Indian Country

One of my friends of the Hopi tribe contacted me, because I had been wanting to get some pictures of the Rain Dance where they carry the rattlesnakes and do all of that, and he told me it was all set up and to come on down.

He said, "You will have to leave your car about a mile and a half below the mesa because you can't get up that narrow way with an automobile. You will have to walk."

I did. They were getting all ready and coming out of the tepees, when I discovered I had forgotten my camera. I told the Chief, I said, "I don't know how I could be that stupid but I have forgotten my camera, and I expect it is gone by now."

He said, "Bill, you don't have to worry. There isn't a white man within eighty miles of here!" *William W. Keeler, Chief Executive Officer, Phillips Petroleum Company*

They Should

The preacher was describing the Day of Judgment: "Lightning will crackle," he said, "thunder will boom; rivers will overflow. Flames will shoot down from the heavens. The earth will quake violently; darkness will fall over the world."

Whereupon a small boy in the front pew piped up to ask his daddy, "Do you think they'll let school out early?"

Did He Believe It?

The speaker was insisting that he made it a rule never to believe anything he could not understand.

"Well, here's something for you to think over," said one of his listeners. "A farmer puts his horse out in the field. The horse eats grass and grows a hair coat. Turning sheep into that same field, they eat the same grass and grow wool coats. Then the geese run in the field and eat the same grass, but they grow feather coats—or don't you believe it?''

Advice

A minister who was a keen, if somewhat erratic, golfer approached the green and was advised by his caddie to use a No. 3 iron. ''I think I can make it with a 4,'' answered the minister. But when the ball landed in a trap short of the green, he commented, ''Well, I guess the good Lord didn't hear me.''

''Could be,'' snapped the caddie, ''but in my church, when we pray, we keep our heads down.''

Modern Youth

The youngster was telling his family about his Sunday school lesson: Moses crossing the Red Sea.

''Moses had his engineers build a pontoon bridge across the sea,'' he related. ''Then his people crossed it. Then his reconnaissance planes radioed and told him an Egyptian tank corps was about to cross the bridge, too. So Moses ordered his jets to blow the bridge up. They did. So Moses and his people were safe.''

''Are you sure that's how your Sunday school teacher told the story?'' asked his father.

''Well, not exactly,'' admitted the boy. ''But the way she told it, you wouldn't believe it.''

Correct

A minister's new secretary, who had formerly worked in the Pentagon, set about reorganizing the minister's filing system.

She labeled one drawer ''Sacred'' and the other ''Top Sacred.''

Sounds Logical

A fourth-grade teacher, discussing heroines from history, asked the class if it knew who Joan of Arc was. ''I think,'' piped a small voice from the rear of the room, ''she was Noah's wife.''

A Hard Question

One of our news commentators in Miami cornered me the other day in the street. He had come alive in his faith in a vital way, and he said, ''John, let me ask you this question: If you were arrested for being a Christian, could they come up with enough evidence to convict you?''

Think about that for a moment: If you were arrested for being a Christian, could they come up with enough evidence to convict you? *John A. Huffman, Jr.*

40

Partners

I remember years ago hearing a story of a little boy who was proud of his garden. I always liked that story because I was a little boy once and I had a garden. The little boy showed his garden to his grandfather and his grandfather complimented him somewhat after this fashion, "Son, you and the Lord have done a mighty good job on that garden." And this bugged the little boy and he wondered, "Grandpa, why what do you mean?" He said, "Well, son, the Lord and you have wrought a great work here. Those are good carrots and that's great corn." The little boy thought awhile, and he thought he would stop grandpa cold, and he said, "But Gramp, you should have seen this garden when God had it by himself!"

The little boy was aware of the fact that he'd been pulling weeds and God hadn't pulled a weed! There were all sorts of things that he could clearly see, for which he was responsible. But he wasn't aware that, as a little boy, he couldn't make one single seed sprout and he couldn't make a seed. He couldn't make the sun shine, he couldn't create water, he hadn't created any of the materials with which he worked. So that while he was indeed a partner with God, without God he couldn't have gotten anywhere with that garden. I suppose it will be a long time before little boys get profound enough in their wisdom to understand things like this. The little boy was right at one point, however. It was vitally important that he give what efforts he had to the whole process. And God demands the same of us. But in addition to the best technical efforts, in addition to our best moral and spiritual commitments, we must depend on God. *Henry H. Mitchell, Sr.*

Obedience

Obedience is not the mark of a slave—it is an important quality in leadership. The great leaders of this world have not been their own masters; they arose and followed someone higher up, and thereby became the greater. Obedience is a gateway to power. Our physical health depends upon obeying the laws of our physical nature. Strength of character issues from obedience to the decree of conscience. If we are to have a commanding hold on life, we must be subject to a will higher than our own.

Words of Wisdom

When young people ask me how they can know God's will for their life, I sometimes answer them that they don't need to know that. If you have a guide whom you trust, you don't need to know the destination to follow Him. So, I say the way to know God's will for your LIFE is to follow Him today—do His will in the present moment because that is the only LIFE you have any promise of. "Commit thy way unto the Lord; trust also in Him; and He shall bring it to pass." (Psalm 37:5). "In ALL thy ways acknowledge Him, and He shall direct thy paths." (Proverbs 3:6). *R. G. LeTourneau, internationally-known manufacturer*

41

Church

In our parish, a hit-and-miss visitor to church was justifying his irregular attendance to our pastor.

"Father, you know what my religion is? It's the Golden Rule," he declaimed proudly. "That's all I need to know about religion."

"You know what my astronomy is?" the priest replied. "It's 'Twinkle, twinkle, little star, how I wonder what you are!' That's all I need to know about astronomy." *Catholic Digest*

Every time we are absent from church we are voting that it shall be closed.

"How many people attend your church," one pastor asked another.

"Sixty regular and about 300 C and E," was the reply.

"C and E?" asked the first.

"Yes, Christmas and Easter."

Be Careful

Be careful how you live. You may be the only Bible some person ever reads.

Faith

David Lilienthal once said, "The essential ingredient of democracy is not doctrine but intelligence, not authority but reason, not cynicism but faith in man, and faith in God. Our strength lies in the fearless pursuit of truth by the minds of men who are free."

Dynamic Faith

We are establishing an all-time world record in the production of material things. What we lack is a righteous and dynamic faith. Without it, all else avails us little. The lack cannot be compensated for by politicians, however able; or by diplomats, however astute; or by scientists, however inventive, or by bombs, however powerful. *John Foster Dulles, former U.S. Secretary of State*

Reading the Bible

I am profitably engaged in reading the Bible. Take all of this Book upon reason that you can, and the balance by faith, and you will live and die a much better man. *Abraham Lincoln*

A Man of Prayer

Washington was known among his soldiers as a man of prayer. It is said on one occasion a visitor to the Continental Congress inquired of Secretary Thomson how he might be able to distinguish Gen. Washington from the other notable men present.

"You can easily pick him out when Congress goes to prayers," the Secretary replied. "Mr. Washington is the man who kneels down when he prays." *William Ward Ayer, Watchman-Examiner*

The Author

Every man's life is a fairy-tale written by God's fingers. *Hans Christian Andersen*

Giving Thanks

No man can really give thanks unless within his heart he deeply feels that undeserved blessings have been bestowed upon him. Our great sin is our carefree assumption that we deserve what God gives and that we are free to do with it what we please. *Calvin H. Wingert*

A Little Bigger

The little boy listened attentively as his father read the scripture lesson for family devotions. He seemed impressed as his parents talked about God's limitless power and mercy.

Then, placing his hands on his father's knees, he asked, "Daddy, how big is God, anyway?"

The man thought for a minute, then said, "Well, son, He's always just a little bit bigger than your need."

Two Dwellings

I will tell you, scholar, I have heard a grave divine say that God has two dwellings, one in heaven and the other in a meek and thankful heart. *Izaak Walton*

The Ways of God

God is subtle but He is not malicious. *Albert Einstein*

A New Day

A traveller in the Swiss Alps spent the night with his guide in a chalet well up in the mountains. In the early hours of the morning he was awakened by terrific crashings and rumblings. Frightened, he aroused his guide and asked, "What is happening? Is the world coming to an end?"

Calmly the guide answered: "No, you see, when the sun starts coming up on the other side of the mountain, its rays touch the snow at the peak, causing it to hurtle down into the valley. Then the warm rays play upon the surface of the glacier and cause the ice to crack with loud reports. It is not the end of the world, only the dawn of a new day!" *Ralph W. Sockman*

A Great Chorale

Probably one of the most famous hymns sung today is the chorale, "A Mighty Fortress Is Our God." Its author, Martin Luther, was a firm believer in congregational singing—he even allowed women to join in public singing! "Satan can smirk, but he cannot laugh; he can sneer, but he cannot sing," he once stated. The year of 1529 was a very discouraging one for this man. Depressed as he had never been, he recalled the stirring words of the 46th Psalm, "God is our refuge and strength, a very present help in trouble." It was then he wrote this great chorale which Joseph Hunecker says "thunders at the very gate of heaven in its magnificent affirmation of beliefs." It spread quickly from country to country and was translated into many languages. The translation most popular in America was written in 1852 by Reverend Frederick H. Hedge, a minister in New England. *Sunshine Magazine*

The Breaks
An elderly matron was mailing her family Bible to a brother in a distant city. The postal clerk examined the large package and inquired if it contained anything breakable.

"Nothing," the lady replied, "but the Ten Commandments."

Two Chances
Man at airline ticket counter: "I'll take two chances on your next flight to Miami."

Similar Experience
The Sunday School teacher was describing how Lot's wife looked back, and turned into a pillar of salt.

Little Johnny was much interested. "My mother looked back once," he explained, "while she was driving, and she turned into a telephone pole!"

Correct
To find out what really happened when the earth was created, engineers spent weeks gathering information, checking and rechecking it, and feeding it into the great computer.

The great moment came. All was complete. Everyone gathered around. A button was punched. The great computer whirled into action. Relays opened and closed. Lights flashed, bells rang.

Finally, a typed message emerged: See Genesis 1:1.

Same Department
The preacher knocked on the door of one of his congregation. "Is that you, Angel?" came a woman's voice.

"No," the minister replied, "but I'm from the same department."

Whoa
A minister sold a mule to a fellow and told him the critter was trained to

go when the rider said "Praise the Lord," and to stop when the rider said, "Amen."

The prospective purchaser mounted the beast, said, "Praise the Lord," and the mule raced away. Becoming excited, the rider kept saying, "Whoa," with no effect on the animal. Then he remembered and said, "Amen."

The mule stopped abruptly. The rider looked down and found the animal had stopped right at the edge of a gigantic cliff. Wiping his brow he declared, gratefully, "Praise the Lord."

He Had Been Praying

An employer, reprimanding a meek employee, said, "Jones, I understand you've been going over my head."

The meek one replied, "Well, sir, I have been praying for a raise."

Have A Merry Christmas

One of the great benefits that comes to us at the Christmas season is the accumulation of wonderful, warm Christmas stories. One story which is tender, a true one, is about a young Presbyterian couple in Brooklyn, New York, Mr. and Mrs. George H. Thomas, Jr. They had a little boy named George who is four years of age. One day they were walking down the street when an old man with a white beard went by them. Little George ran after him and tugged on his coattail, and he said, "Santa, will you please bring me a teddy-bear for Christmas?" The parents were embarrassed. The old man just wryly winked at the boy, patted him on the head, and went on his way. On Christmas morning there was a knock on the door even before little George was out of bed. And here stood the old man, white beard and all, with a teddy-bear in his hand. He gave it to the surprised young parents and he simply said, "I didn't want the little fellow to be disappointed." As he walked on back down the steps they said, "Good-by, Rabbi Podolsky. Have a Merry Christmas." It's a warm story. A time like this is one that warms our hearts and brings us closer together, and surely if there ever was a time in a broken world when we needed that, it's today. *Ernest J. Lewis*

Confident

MINISTER: Johnny, don't you say prayers before eating?
JOHNNY: No, sir, I don't need to; my mother's a good cook.

Ants

The ant preaches a good sermon and she does it without saying anything.

On a picnic you are soon convinced that Noah had more than two ants in the ark.

Because

Because I have seen the flowers,
I know what color is . . .
what fragrance is . . .
what beauty is . . .

Because I have seen the springtime's
divine awakening,
I know what hope is . . .
what faith is . . .
what joy is . . .

Because I have seen the eagle soar
and the tall pines swaying in the breeze,
I know what grace is . . .

Because I have listened to the birds
carol at daybreak,
I know what gladness is . . .
what thanksgiving is . . .

Because I have seen the seeds
reveal their wonders in radiant life,
I know what mystery is . . .

Because I have looked upon the mountain,
the ocean, and the trees,
I know what majesty is . . .
what grandeur is . . .
what repose is . . .

Because I have seen the sun,
the moon, and the stars in their
ponderous courses,
I know what power is . . .

Contemplation of these revelations
Mounts faith almost to understanding.
Author unknown

Noise

There would be far less noise in the world if people talked as seldom as they prayed.

Einstein's Belief

I cannot believe that God plays dice with the cosmos. *Albert Einstein*

Let It Be So . . .

May the road rise to meet you,
May the wind be always at your back,
May the sun shine warm upon your face,
The rains fall soft upon your fields,
And until we meet again, may God hold you
In the palm of His hand.

Old Gaelic Blessing

My Father's World

This is my Father's world,
And to my listening ears
All nature sings, and round me rings
The music of the spheres,
This is my Father's world,
I rest me in the thought
Of rocks and trees, of skies and seas
His hand the wonders wrought.

More about Lincoln and Prayer

It happened during the early hours of the battle of Gettysburg. In the White House Abraham Lincoln was pacing up and down, lonely and troubled, as the battle reports poured in and the fate of the United States hung in the balance. At that time when everybody seemed panic-stricken, Lincoln went to his room and locked the door. One can picture him there down on his knees, his great head in his hands, praying like a child. Later Lincoln described that moment to a friend in this fashion:

"I told God that I had done all that I could and that now the result was in His hands; that if this country was to be saved, it was because He so willed it. The burden fell off my shoulders, my intense anxiety was relieved, and in its place came a great trustfulness!" *Sunshine Magazine*

Righteousness

One thing familiarity doesn't breed contempt for is righteousness.

The Golden Rule

You seldom hear of a mob rushing across town to support the Golden Rule.

There is no substitute for the Golden Rule—not even brass.

Spare Tire

Many treat their religion like a spare tire—they never use it except in an emergency.

Church News

Sign on church bulletin board: "This is the gateway to Heaven. Closed during July and August."

Notice in a church bulletin: "Come to the morning service early if you want a good back seat."

If you go to church by proxy, you should be willing to go to heaven the same way.

Faith

I propose that God should be openly and audibly invoked at the United Nations in accordance with any one of the religious faiths which are represented here. I do so in the conviction that we cannot make the United Nations into a successful instrument of God's peace without God's help—and that with His help we cannot fail. *Henry Cabot Lodge, Jr., one-time chief U.S. delegate to the United Nations*

God Bless Us Every One

All the blessed sentiments of Christmas dwell in these words of Tiny Tim. Good will is there, gratitude to God, the soulful sense of the brotherhood of man, that divine spark of unselfishness which glows supreme in the Yuletide, though it may be smothered with ashes in all the rest of the year.

"Every one" allows no exceptions. The rich, the poor, the kind, the cruel, the good, the bad—all are included. All do not deserve the divine blessing equally, but all need it equally, and in their several ways may be touched and purified and lifted up, for the moment at least, to a realization of the spiritual meaning of life. *Sunshine Magazine*

6

No Place Like Home

Not Tough
The rookie hillbilly had just run his first obstacle course in the Marines.

"Well, Zeke," the drill sergeant said, "what do you think of the Marines now?"

"Shucks, it's really nothin', Sarge," the hillbilly answered. "Where I come from, we go through country like that jest to get to the barn."

Sure Sign
Boy Scout leader to the troops: "Remember, fellows, if you're lost in the woods at night, get your bearings from the sky. A glow will indicate the nearest shopping center."

Fishing
Some people insist a fishing pole is a stick with a worm on both ends of it.

Mistaken Identity
A meek little man in a restaurant timidly touched the arm of a man putting on a coat.

"Excuse me," he said, "but do you happen to be Mr. Smith of New-castle?"

"No, I'm not!" the man answered impatiently.

"Oh—er—well," stammered the first man, "you see, I am, and that's his coat you're putting on."

Tidbit
If you can look in the mirror without laughing, you have no sense of humor.

Little Things
If you don't think little things are important, try sitting on a tack.

When you see a man about to sit on a tack, it is a sign of an early spring.

Not Safe

Robert Benchley heartily disliked the outdoors. He went to great pains to avoid fresh air.

One cloudless day in Hollywood, a friend called on the humorist and found him sunning himself under a lamp.

"Why are you sitting under that?" demanded the friend. He pointed to the sun-drenched lawn outside the window. "Why don't you sit out there?"

Said Benchley, recoiling, "And get hit by a meteor?" *Milwaukee Journal*

It Was Longer

"Are you the barber who cut my hair last time?" asked the rock-n-roll singer as he seated himself in the chair.

"It couldn't have been me," said the barber, "I've only been here six months."

Taking No Chances

Two caterpillars were crawling across the grass when a butterfly flew over them. They looked up, and one nudged the other and said: "You couldn't get me up in one of those things for a million dollars!"

Was That Nice

A fellow at a cocktail party asked the wife of one of the noisier guests, "What does your husband want to be when he grows up?"

For fixing things around the house, nothing beats a man who's handy with a checkbook.

My Hope

By profession I am a soldier, and take pride in that fact. But I am more proud, infinitely more, to be a father. A soldier destroys in order to build; a father only builds, never destroys. The one has the potentialities of death, the other embodies creation and life. While the hordes of death are mighty, the battalions of life are mightier still. It is my hope that my son, when I am gone, will remember me not from the battles, but in the home, repeating with him our simple daily prayer, "Our Father, who art in heaven." *General Douglas MacArthur*

Parents

A baby's cry in the night has great carrying power, and Dad is generally the carrier.

It's almost impossible to train children at home without having the parents there at some time.

No Use

"When the boy threw stones at you," the mother scolded her son, "why didn't you come and tell me instead of throwing stones back at him?"

"What good would that do?" asked the boy. "You couldn't hit the side of a barn."

Plenty to Live for

Wife to depressed husband: "What do you mean you have nothing to live for? The house isn't paid for, the car isn't paid for, the washing machine isn't paid for, the television isn't paid for . . ."

Christmas Past

Wife explaining February bills to mate: "The ghost of Christmas past!"

The Family Circle

Since we have done away with the old family album, what will our grandchildren have to laugh at?

Many of the homes nowadays seem to be on three shifts—father is on the night shift, mother is on the day shift, and the children shift for themselves.

Former Senator Kenneth B. Keating had this letter from the parent of a teenager: "Now that my son has a driver's license, I always know where he is. The only trouble is, I don't know where the car is."

Open in Terror

He had installed automatic garage doors. "Do they really work?" he was asked. "They sure do," he said. "My teenagers don't even have to push the button. When they see them coming up the driveway, they fly open in sheer terror!"

Aren't They All?

FIRST TEENAGER (*bragging a bit*): My room is decorated in Country French Style.

SECOND TEENAGER: Mine is done in Danish Modern.

THIRD TEENAGER: Mine is in contemporary disorder.

Thoughtful

A father, putting a fifty-foot extension cord on the telephone, explained, "Now that the weather is nice, I want my daughter to stay outdoors more."

The Answers

I don't pretend to have all the answers. If I did, I'd be a college freshman.

Of Course

Believing that today's children are overindulged, a father became furious when his teenage son asked to be driven three blocks to school.

"'Drive you to school?" the father exclaimed. "Why do you suppose you have two feet?"

To which the boy replied, "Isn't one to put on the brake and the other to put on the accelerator?"

Return Department—Please Note

Teenager to a clothing salesman: "If my parents like this, can I return it?"

Couldn't Help It

Teenager's apology to friend: You'll have to excuse the way my room looks. My folks made me clean it up.

This We Want to Hear

It will be interesting to hear today's teenagers tell their own children what they had to do without.

Modern Youth

The father was scolding his teenage daughter for her sloven appearance. "You modern girls don't seem to care how you look any more," he declared. "Why, your hair looks like a mop."

"What's a mop?" the daughter inquired innocently.

Too Late

Why can't life's problems hit us when we are eighteen and know everything?

Short Wait

Father (to daughter's boyfriend): "She will be right down. Care for a game of chess?"

Ignorant

Senior citizen to friend: "I survived World War II, three auto accidents, two bad marriages, two depressions, 13 company strikes, three mortgages, and the government farm policies—and a fresh teenager tells me I don't know what life is all about!"

A Boy

How is it that the boy who wasn't good enough to marry your daughter can become the father of the smartest grandchildren in the world?

A boy is a magical creature—you can lock him out of your workshop, but you can't lock him out of your heart. You can get him out of your study, but you can't get him out of your mind. Might as well give up—he is your captor, your jailer, your boss, your master—a freckled-faced, pint-sized, cat-chasing bundle of noise. But when you come home at night with only the shattered pieces of your hopes and dreams, he can mend them like new with two magic words—"Hi, Dad!" *Alan Beck, "What Is a Boy?"*

A Girl
Little girls are the nicest things that happen to people. They are born with a little bit of angelshine about them and though it wears thin sometimes there is always enough left to lasso your heart—even when they are sitting in the mud, or crying temperamental tears, or parading up the street in mother's best clothes. *Alan Beck, "What Is a Girl?"*

The Home
Good, honest, hardheaded character is a function of the home. If the proper seed is sown there and properly nourished for a few years, it will not be easy for that plant to be uprooted. *George A. Dorsey*

Family
Your life may be more pleasant and peaceful when at last you decide that what your relatives do is none of your business.

When some families can make the down payment on it, a luxury becomes a necessity.

By the time a family gets the suitcases packed and the car loaded they need a vacation.

Home Sweet Home
A good many homes are still without bathtubs, but after all, a good many people seldom stay home.

The man who lives in a house by the side of the road now is in a trailer.

If you buy a summer cottage, your friends will have a place to spend their weekends.

Everyone should travel to become acquainted with the comforts of home.

We're glad the old woman who lived in a shoe existed long years ago. It wouldn't be fun to live in a home with an open heel and toe.

Every suburbanite who has tried to make grass grow stands in awe of a farmer.

Crabgrass: A plant that will take a yard if you give it an inch.

In a pre-fabricated home you get everything except a family.

Take One

Gas and electric company servicemen are used to finding notes from customers advising of various pets to be encountered in the house. But this note caused a man to do a doubletake—and this was all he took!

The note read: "Furnace is in the hallway—do service. Dogs are in the kitchen—do avoid. Guinea pig in hallway—do not squash. Cats everywhere—do take one home."

Not Bad

WILLIE: I fell off a sixty-foot ladder today.

CHARLEY: Goodness! Were you hurt?

WILLIE: Naw, I only fell off the first rung.

As the departing geranium said to the bright red rose, "Ile B. Zinnia."

As the world grows more civilized, we keep right on improving padlocks.

Enjoying the Music

A lady appeared before a judge and complained angrily against the people next door.

"What's the trouble?" asked the judge.

"Every night this week they have been pounding on the wall and yelling at me until two o'clock in the morning!"

"Dear, dear!" exclaimed the judge. "And does the noise keep you awake?"

"No," explained the lady, "but I can't enjoy my piano playing with all that noise going on."

Tough Neighborhood

A tough neighborhood is one in which any cat with a tail is a tourist.

Sometimes you have to call a spade a spade to get it back from your neighbor.

A rummage sale is where you buy some junk from other people's attics to put in your own attic.

Rumors

People don't always believe everything they hear, but often repeat it just to be on the safe side.

Debt

A lot of people go into debt just to keep up with their friends who already are.

Alas

Never make little of yourself. Your friends will do it for you.

Small Town

Mark Twain visited Windsor many years ago, and the local Chamber of Commerce people showed him the attractions of the Windsor area. They showed him the river, first when the tide was in, and then when the tide was out.

They asked him what he thought of it, and it is local legend that Mark Twain is reputed to have said that never before had he realized how important water was to a river.

One would have thought that they would have left well enough alone, but they pressed the matter further and said, "Well, Mr. Twain, what do you think of Windsor itself?"

Finally, after finding himself thoroughly cornered, Mark Twain said he would have to grant that Windsor was a unique town. He was questioned further as to what he meant by *unique*: "What do you mean? In what way is Windsor a unique town?"

Mark Twain said that he supposed that when he said Windsor was a unique town that he had in mind the derivation from the Latin *uni* which is "one," and *ques* meaning "horse." *Gerald A. Regan*

A small town baseball league is one in which the choice of pitchers depends on the collection before the game.

The Good Old Days

In the old days a horse had sense enough to take a second look at a railroad crossing.

We speak longingly of the good old days because we know we won't have to live through them again.

We always feel sad when we see a horsefly sitting on a truck radiator.

Buffet Suppers

A buffet supper is something a person lives through in order to get to bed.

Not Taking a Chance

"Tell me what you eat, and I'll tell you what you are," said a lunch-counter philosopher. Whereupon a meek little man, sitting a few stools away, whispered to the waitress, "Cancel my order for shrimp salad."

Fast Eaters

"You fellows are the fastest eaters I ever saw," said Bob Hope. "I lowered my head to say grace, and when I looked up the cook asked me what I wanted for dessert."

We suppose the reason hot dogs are so popular is that it's almost impossible for a cook to ruin them.

Scientists say mosquitoes can travel long distances. Yes, but they stop for refreshments.

We suppose it's because most restaurants have expanded that the portions look so small.

We sometimes wonder if nature really made prunes more healthful than strawberries.

Don't Blame Them

A Congressman out in Wyoming, told of a bear that wandered into a bar out there, sat down on a bar stool, ordered a beer, and put a five dollar bill down on the bar.

The bartender was nonplussed. He uncorked the beer, took the five dollars, and went in the backroom to see the boss. He said, "Boss, you won't believe what just happened. A bear walked in here and ordered a beer. He laid a five dollar bill on the bar. What should I do?"

The boss said, "Well, give him a nickel change. Bears aren't very smart."

So he went back out, put the nickel change on the bar, and the bear said nothing, but continued to nurse his beer quietly.

Finally, the curiosity of the bartender was overpowering, so he walked around to the other side of the bar and sat on the stool next to the bear, and he said, "You know, we don't get too many bears in here."

The bear said, "At $4.95 a beer I can see why." *Philip M. Crane, Congressman*

Worst One We've Heard

The most unfortunate person we know is the soda jerk who was fired for flunking his fizzicle.

Films

A man took his dog to a movie house and sat it in the seat beside him. The usherette was going to throw the dog out until she noticed that it was paying close attention to the film. After the movie, she went to the man and said, "It really amazed me to see your dog enjoying the picture."

"Amazed me, too," said the man. "He didn't like the book."

Too Long

Some films end happily, but not soon enough.

A Suggestion

A concert had been arranged and all the stars in the city were booked to appear.

Miss Handbloom, the favorite soprano, was to sing, and, before she began, she apologized for her cold. Then she sang: "I'll hang my harp on a willow tree-e-e. Ahem!"

"On a willow tree-e-e-. Oh!"

Her voice broke on the high note each time. She tried it again. Then a voice came from the rear of the hall: "Try hanging it on a lower branch, lady."

Easy to Entertain

It is easy to entertain some people. All you have to do is just sit down and listen.

Exercise

"There's nothing like getting up at six in the morning, going for a run around the park, and taking a quick shower before breakfast," said Tom enthusiastically.

"How long have you been doing this?" asked Bob.

"I start tomorrow."

Better Off

There's nothing like the first horseback ride to make a person feel better off.

Keep Busy

The husband was a fanatic on the subject of physical fitness. After much persuasion, he finally got his wife to go jogging with him, but she soon twisted her ankle and sank to the ground, groaning.

"Don't worry, honey," her husband assured her. "I'm off to get help. But while we're waiting for the ambulance, don't just lie there. Couldn't you do a few push-ups?"

Typical
Golf is a game where you sock the ball hard and walk four feet.

Long Wait
The doctor's waiting room was full. Every chair was taken; some patients were even standing. There was a desultory conversation, but after a while silence fell. The patients waited.

Finally an old man stood up wearily and remarked: "Well, I guess I'll go home and die a natural death."

Calm
A doctor says those tranquilizer pills work so well that some of his patients don't care whether they pay him or not.

A Rule Is a Rule
A new patient was quite upset when the doctor's nurse led him to a small curtained cubicle and told him to undress.

"But I only want the doctor to look at an ingrown toenail!" he protested.

"Our rule is that everyone undresses," snapped the nurse as she left him.

"A foolish rule," grumbled the patient as he complied. "Making me undress just to look at my toe."

"That's nothing," growled a voice from the next cubicle. "I came in to fix the telephone!"

How It Works
A neurotic builds air castles. A psychotic lives in them. A psychoanalyst collects the rent.

No Repetition
A proud father phoned the newspaper and reported the birth of twins. The girl at the desk didn't quite catch the message.

"Will you repeat that?" she asked.

"Not if I can help it," he replied.

Rest
The noted physician was examining a noted actress. "There's nothing seriously wrong with you," he said. "You just need rest."

"But, you didn't even look at my tongue."

"I didn't need to," said the doctor. "It needs rest, too."

Understandable
Hospital patient receiving bill for an operation: "No wonder they wore masks in the operating room."

Good for the Heart

It is good for the hearts of men, as of women, to do their own chores, to cut the grass, to shovel the snow, to dig and weed the garden . . . it gets us down to earth, keeps us humble, is good for our health, and, incidentally, saves us money. *Dr. Paul Dudley White, heart specialist*

Gardening

The principal objection to gardening is that by the time your back gets used to it, your enthusiasm is gone.

Not the Defendant

The judge read the charges, then asked, "Are you the defendant in this case?"

"No sir, your honor," came the reply, "I've got a lawyer to do the defendin'. I'm the guy who done it."

Cooler Tomorrow

MAGISTRATE: Driving through the red light will cost you $10 and costs, and next time you'll go to jail. Understand?

CULPRIT: Yes, your Honor, just like a weather report—fine today, cooler tomorrow.

Not Taking a Chance

In a country courtroom, the bailiff escorted a little, old gray-haired lady to the witness stand and swore her in.

He asked, "Are you acquainted with the prosecuting attorney?"

She replied, "Yes, I know him quite well, and he's a crook!"

Next he asked if she were acquainted with the defending attorney.

"Yes", she nodded, "I know him, and he's a crook, too!"

The judge beckoned to the bailiff and whispered in his ear: "If you ask her if she knows me, I'll have you arrested for contempt of court."

Bumper Sticker

Things are being threshed out by bumper stickers these days. I saw one the other day that said, "Ralph Nader is defective."

Then I saw one that said, "Disregard the message on the front bumper."

One fellow said to me, "I completely disagree with your bumper sticker, but I'll fight for your right to stick it."

7

Good Thinking

That's Different

Two men were trying to measure a flagpole. After they had made guesses that differed considerably, a bystander asked, "Wouldn't it be easier to lay the pole on the ground and measure how long it is?"

"No," replied one of the men. "We are trying to figure out how tall it is, not how long it is."

He Needed Practice

Grandmother was trying to teach Tommy good manners. After a few lessons, Tommy asked, "Grandma, If I'm invited out to dinner should I eat pie with a fork?"

"Yes, indeed, Tommy," was the reply.

"Well, Grandma," mused Tommy, "do you have a piece of pie in the house that I could practice on?"

Good Question

Seven year old to father: "Before you married Mom, who told you how to drive?"

One Way of Stating It

"Daddy, did you win?" his two youngsters asked when Al Burgin returned home from a round of golf.

"Well, children," replied Burgin, "in golf it doesn't matter so much if you win. But your father got to hit the ball more times than anyone else."

Reasonable

A man had barely paid off his mortgage on the house when he mortgaged it again to buy a car, and then borrowed money to build a garage. "If I do make the loan," said the banker, "how will you buy gas for the car?"

"It seems to me," the man replied curtly, "that a fellow who owns his own house, a car and garage should be able to get credit for gasoline."

We All Do

An old farmer was walking along talking earnestly to himself.

A neighbor called to him and said, "Hey, there, Henry, why are you talking to yourself?"

"First," replied the farmer, "I like to hear a smart man talk, and next, I like to talk to a smart man."

Fast Thinking

MR. NEWLYWED: Do you mean there's only cheese for dinner?

MRS. NEWLYWED: Yes, dear. When the chops caught fire and fell into the dessert, I had to use the soup to put out the fire.

Understandable

During World War II, a buck private and a sergeant were courtmartialed for striking a colonel.

Asked why he had done it, the sergeant explained that the colonel, while passing down the line of review, had stepped on his sore foot.

"Instinctively," said the sergeant, "I threw up my guard, like anyone would do, and let him have it before I realized what had actually happened. It was an accident, I can assure you."

Then the buck private was asked for his explanation. "Well, you see, sir," he replied, "when I saw the sergeant strike the colonel, I thought the war was over."

Smart

A young woman and a handsome farm lad were walking along a country road one evening. The farm lad was carrying a large pail on his back, holding a chicken in one hand, a cane in the other and leading a goat. They came to a long dark lane.

Said the girl: "I'm afraid to walk here with you. You might try to kiss me."

Said the farm lad: "How could I, with all these things I'm carrying?"

"Well, you might stick the cane in the ground, tie the goat to it, and put the chicken under the pail."

Smart Computer

"What's wrong with the computer?" asked the office manager.

"Someone dropped a rubber band in it and it's been making snap decisions," replied the programmer.

Propriety

One night at a very conservative old club for men, a dignified member walked in and was shocked to see women there for the first time. "We've decided to let members bring their wives in for dinner and dancing," the manager informed him.

"But I'm not married," complained the member. "Could I bring a girl friend?"

The manager thought for a minute and replied: "I think it might be all right, provided she's the wife of a member."

61

Modern History

When the teacher asked her first-graders what they knew about George Washington, one little girl offered:

"George Washington was a very bad boy. He cut down a cherry tree and his father spanked him until he couldn't sit down." She paused for breath.

"And that," she concluded, "is why he stood up in the boat."

Sorry I Complained

CUSTOMER: Waiter, I can't find any oysters in this oyster stew.

WAITER: "Well, you wouldn't expect to find any angels in angel food cake, would you?"

Tough Question

After giving what he considered a stirring, fact-filled campaign speech, the candidate looked out at his audience and confidently asked: "Are there any questions?"

"Yes," came a voice from the rear. "Who else is running?"

Is That Clear?

FOREIGNER (*in drugstore*): No, I want the small size.

CLERK: In America, sir, there are only three sizes: large, giant, and super. If you want small, take the large.

The Small Car

An alarmed motorist stopped hurriedly when he saw a young man standing beside an overturned small sports car. "Anybody hurt in the accident?" he inquired.

"There wasn't any accident," replied the young man calmly, "I'm changing a tire."

A Lot of Them

The story is told of a drill sergeant who barked a command: "All right, you dummies, fall out!"

With much confusion and clatter, every man in the company except one fell out and scattered. The sergeant glared at the remaining recruit and said, "Well?"

The rookie smiled and replied, "There sure were a lot of them, weren't there, Sarge?"

Ten O'Clock News

Weather forecaster to radio announcer: "Better break it to them gently. Just say, 'Partly cloudy, somewhat cooler, with heavy local showers, followed by a hurricane.'"

Obvious Answer

No trait is more useful in life than the ability to laugh at one's own defects—just as Abraham Lincoln was able to make fun of his homeliness. Once during a debate Douglas accused him of being two-faced. Replied Lincoln calmly: "I leave it to my audience—if I had two faces, would I be wearing this one?"

That's Different

The defense counsel was cross-examining the police officer who had arrested his client for drunkenness. "The fact that a man is on his hands and knees in the middle of the road," argued the lawyer, "doesn't constitute proof that he was intoxicated."

"I agree, sir," the policeman politely acknowledged, "but this guy was trying to roll up the white line."

Prescription

The doctor explained to an overweight patient, "These pills I'm prescribing for you are not to be swallowed. You just spill them on the floor twice a day and pick them up one at a time."

No Use

It was an ordinary home without a maid and seldom a guest. Therefore when Dad appeared with two dinner guests, the young son was anxious to help his mother.

When dinner was nearly over, the boy went to the kitchen and carried in the first piece of apple pie, giving it to his father, who passed it to a guest.

The boy came came in with a second piece of pie and gave it to his father who again gave it to a guest.

This was too much for the boy, who said, "It's no use, Dad. The pieces are all the same size."

Forecasting

In 1900, a writer in *The New York Times* prophesied that the advent of the automobile would solve the parking problem, since the auto occupies less space at a curb than a horse and wagon.

Good Argument

The hotel clerk was losing his patience, and so was the gentleman trying to get a room. "Look, Mr. Smith," said the clerk, "I've told you a dozen times already we don't have any rooms. We're full!"

"If the President of the United States came in," Smith persisted, "you'd have a room for him, wouldn't you?"

"Why, of course," the clerk admitted readily.

"Then let me have his room," said Smith. "He's not coming."

How to Get in Shape

The 97-pound weakling, tired of being ignored by the girls and bullied by the big guys, sent away for a set of barbells and other weight-lifting body-builders. After several weeks, a friend asked how he was coming with his personal physical fitness program.

"Just fine," replied the little fellow. "I'm getting pretty good at lifting those bars. In a few weeks I hope I can start putting the round things on the ends of them."

Thrifty

Improvident Joe said to the grocer one day, "I gotta have a few groceries. We're starvin'!"

"Well, all right, Joe," said the grocer, "if you haven't any money, I'll give you a sackful. But you'd better not sell them and take your family to the circus tomorrow."

"Oh, no," promised Joe. "I got the circus money saved up already."

Taught Him a Lesson

An elderly woman went to the racetrack with friends and placed a $2 bet—the first of her life—on a long shot whose name appealed to her.

Her horse won and paid 18 to 1. As the clerk at the cashier's window handed the woman her winnings, she frowned disapprovingly and admonished him: "I hope this will be a lesson to you, young man!"

Of Course

The man who thinks he knows it all is a pain in the neck to those of us who really do.

Understandable

A troop of Boy Scouts was being used as "guinea pig" in a civil defense test. The mock air raid was staged, and the Scouts impersonated wounded persons who were to be picked up and cared for by the defense units. One Scout was supposed to lie on the ground and await his rescuers, but the first-aid people got behind schedule, and the Scout lay "wounded" for several hours. When the first-aid squad arrived where the casualty was supposed to be, they found nothing but a brief note: "Have bled to death and gone home."

That's Different

A girl approached an old gentleman and asked him to buy a chance on a turkey.

"No," he said, "I can't eat turkey—doesn't agree with me."

"But," argued the lass, "don't forget, you aren't likely to win it."

"Well, I never thought of that," he replied. "Give me ten tickets!"

64

The Help Was No Good

The boss came along and ordered one of the men to dig a hole eight feet deep. After the job was completed the boss returned and explained that an error had been made and the hole would not be needed. "Fill 'er up," he commanded.

The worker did as he'd been told. But he ran into a problem. He couldn't get all the dirt packed back into the hole without leaving a mound on top. He went to the office and explained his problem.

The boss snorted. "The kind of help you get these days! There's only one thing to do. You'll have to dig that hole deeper!"

Certainly

The querulous customer, examining a cowhide jacket, demanded, "Are you sure this is good material?"

"Of course," replied the clerk, "it held the cow together."

Fair Enough

Sign on a sanitation truck: "Satisfaction guaranteed—or double your garbage back."

Pluck

It really takes pluck for a woman to shape her eyebrows.

Poverty

The late Chief Justice Earl Warren came from a home where even the necessities were in short supply. Once, when he was a boy, he asked his father why he hadn't been given a middle name.

"Son," his father told him, "when you were born, we couldn't afford that kind of luxury."

Could Be

Two dogs were talking. "What's your name?" asked the first.

"I'm not sure," replied the second, "but I think it must be Down Boy!"

That Does It!

At a neighborhood barbecue the local bully sauntered over to his new neighbor, a small slight man, and chopped him across the shoulders. While the little guy struggled to his feet, the big guy said, "That's karate, got it in Japan."

A few minutes later, he grabbed the small fellow again, hurled him over his shoulder and said, "That's judo, got it in Japan."

The new neighbor had all he could take and left. Returning later in the evening, he walked up behind the bully, cracked him over the head and said, "That's crowbar, got it at Sears!"

Sorry, Officer

It had rained hard, and the windshield was so spattered with mud that the car narrowly missed several collisions. The enraged motorcycle policeman curbed the car and asked, "Lady, don't you think it would help some to clean off your windshield?"

"I don't believe so, Officer," came the cheery reply. "I left my glasses at home today."

Just Thinking

The art of meditation may be exercised at all hours and in all places; and men of genius, in their walks, at table, and amidst assemblies, turning the eye of the mind inwards, can form an artificial solitude—retire amidst a crowd, be calm amidst distraction, and wise amidst folly. *Isaac Disraeli*

Sage Advice

The ancient sage who concocted the maxim, "Know thyself," should have added: "Don't tell anyone."

Tolerance

Always be tolerant with those who disagree with you. They have a right to their ridiculous opinions.

Misers

A miser might be pretty tough to live with, but he's a nice ancestor.

Heroes

The people you figure are men of steel may just be solid brass.

Marvelous Mechanism

The human brain, which weighs only about three pounds, is pretty small. But—it has more than ten billion parts; it is portable so we can take it with us wherever we go; it can be taught almost anything; it builds computers to save thinking time; it can plan ahead; it understands the Ten Commandments. Yes, the human brain is the most expertly-designed mechanism devised.

God and Man

A farmer whose corn crop hadn't done well, decided to "borrow" from his prosperous neighbor's field. With a large sack tucked under his arm, and his small son dogging his footsteps, he hurried to a distant corner of the field.

On arrival, he peered cautiously to the left, to the right, ahead and behind, to make sure he was not observed.

Just as he reached out a hand to pluck the first ear of corn, the lad spoke: "Daddy," he reminded, "you didn't look up!" *Ruth A. Pray*

Last One Up

As a rule, ministers do not draw illustrations from prize fights; but bishops must look into a number of matters if they are to advise the clergy what to avoid. Some years ago two individuals were to fight for the so-called heavyweight championship of the world. One was an Italian, named Carnera, better known for bulk than brains. The other was Max Baer, with a propensity for wisecracking, who was at home upon the vaudeville stage. In the midst of that fight, each swung at the other, each missed, each fell to the canvas, and the crowds witnessed the sorry spectacle of two fighters lying in the middle of the ring, facing each other. Before Carnera could rise, Baer grinned and said, "The last one up is a sissy." It may be necessary for us to repeat that line today. "The last one up is a sissy." *Bishop G. Bromley Oxnam*

Trouble

It's strange how trouble often starts out being fun.

Even Better

Being alert to speak is important, but being silent at the right time is even better.

Boners

And there was the freshman in engineering who thought that steel wool was the fleece of an hydraulic ram.

John Veneman, Undersecretary of Health, Education and Welfare during the first Nixon term, told of the hard-pressed football team that finally got possession of the ball on its own three-yard line. The coach decided to try a new, young quarterback, and sent him in with instructions to "run play 22-E twice, and then punt."

The quarterback called play 22-E and miraculously made 45 yards. He called it again, and this time made 49. With the ball on the opponents' five, he then punted. As he came off the field, the coach grabbed him and angrily asked, "Just what was going through your mind on that last play?"

"The only thing going through my mind," answered the quarterback, "was, man, have we ever got a dumb coach!" *From a column by Alan L. Otten in the Wall Street Journal*

Never Mind

Our Postmaster reports this label on a box of fish: "If not delivered in ten days, never mind."

Improves with Time

Nothing improves with time like a person's opinion of himself.

Praise

Praise is never heard by those to whom it is generally given—the dead.

Overweight?

Never admit that you are fat. Just say you come in the large economy size.

Just a Partial Job

DENTIST: Your teeth are in bad shape; you should have a bridge put in at once.

PATIENT: What would it cost?

DENTIST: Oh, about $175.

PATIENT: Couldn't you put in just a culvert now?

Technology

What we want is an electrical gadget that pays the electric bill.

Squares

There is one thing you have to say for a square and that is that he doesn't think in circles.

Sorry

An old lady was having her eyes examined. The optician placed some cards at a distance, with the letters XZPTVCH and asked her if she could see them clearly. Said she: "I can see them clearly, but I can't read Russian."

That Will Hold Them

"Your honor," said the first lawyer, "I am opposed by an unmitigated scoundrel."

Said the second lawyer, "My learned friend is notorious—"

The judge interrupted sharply, "Counsel will kindly confine their remarks to such matters as are in dispute."

Dress

One of Mark Twain's bad habits, in the eyes of his wife, was his custom of calling on neighbors without a collar or necktie. One afternoon upon his return from a neighborhood visit, his wife scolded him for his negligence. So Clemens departed to his study and in a few moments sent a small package back to the neighbor's house. An accompanying note read as follows:

"Just a little while ago I visited you for something like a half-hour minus my collar and tie. The missing articles are enclosed. Will you kindly gaze at them for 30 minutes and then return them to me?"

Baseball

"Where's your dog?"

"I have no dog," replied the umpire. "Why?"

"Well, you're the first blind man I ever saw without a dog."

Correct

"I can tell you the baseball score before it starts." "What is it?" "Nothing to nothing—before it starts!"

Playing Zoo

Tommy was an ambitious youngster. "Mother," he exclaimed, "Billy and I are playing zoo. We're going to be elephants and we want you to play."

"What can I do?" asked mother.

"Well, you can be the lady who feeds the elephants peanuts."

Discouraging

We suppose a hen gets discouraged because she always find things missing from where she laid them.

Privilege of a Fisherman

Saint Peter stopped a man who knocked at the Gates of Heaven.

"You have told too many lies to get in here," said the Keeper of the Keys.

"Have a heart, Saint Peter," said the new arrival. "You were a fisherman once yourself."

Don't Keep Smiling

If you "keep smiling," some people are going to wonder what you have been up to.

Faults

All of us can live happily with our own faults, but living with the faults of others is almost impossible.

Playing It Safe

Mark Twain, in his reporting days, was instructed by an editor never to state anything as a fact that he could not verify from personal knowledge. Sent out to cover an important social event soon afterward, he turned in the following:

"A woman giving the name of Mrs. James Jones, who is reported to be one of the society leaders of the city, is said to have given what purported to be a party yesterday to a number of alleged ladies. The hostess claims to be the wife of a reputed attorney."

Too Big to Lose

The schoolteacher was giving her young pupils a test in natural history.

"Now, Dick," she said, "tell me where the elephant is found."

Dick hesitated. Then his face lit up. "The elephant," he said, "is such a large animal, it is scarcely ever lost."

Foreigners Don't Count

"Who was the first man, Bobby?" asked the teacher.

"George Washington," answered Bobby promptly.

"Why, no, Bobby," exclaimed the teacher. "You ought to know better. Adam was the first man."

"Oh, well," said Bobby, determined to prove himself right, "I wasn't counting foreigners."

If There Is

The Chinese have a proverb, in fact a precept, which if carried to fruition would cure the ills of the world. It is this:

"If there is righteousness in the heart, there will be beauty in the character. If there is beauty in the character, there will be harmony in the home. If there is harmony in the home, there will be order in the nation. If there is order in the nation, there will be peace in the world."

8

Humorous Quotations of Famous Persons

If a man keeps his trap shut, the world will beat a path to his door. *Franklin Pierce Adams*

Early to bed and early to rise, and you'll meet very few of our best people. *George Ade*

For parlor use, the vague generality is a lifesaver. *George Ade*

The English instinctively admire any man who has no talent and is modest about it. *James Agate*

He had insomnia so bad that he couldn't sleep when he was working. *Arthur Baer*

She's generous to a fault—if it's her own. *Arthur Baer*

Nobody can be exactly like me. Sometimes even I have trouble doing it. *Tallulah Bankhead*

Drawing on my fine command of language, I said nothing. *Robert Benchley*

It was one of those plays in which all the actors unfortunately enunciated very clearly. *Robert Benchley*

Do you realize if it weren't for Edison we'd be watching TV by candlelight? *Al Boliska*

Adam invented love at first sight, one of the greatest labor-saving machines the world ever saw. *Josh Billings*

The best way to convince a fool that he is wrong is to let him have his own way. *Josh Billings*

No man is so poor that he can't afford to keep one dog, and I've seen them so poor that they could afford to keep three. *Josh Billings*

For those who do not think, it is best at least to rearrange their prejudices once in a while. *Luther Burbank*

Middle age is when your old classmates are so grey and wrinkled and bald they don't recognize you. *Bennett Cerf*

He's all buttoned up in an impenetrable little coat of complacency. *Ilka Chase*

The less one has to do, the less time one finds to do it in. *Lord Chesterfield*

Most people enjoy the inferiority of their best friends. *Lord Chesterfield*

Optimism: The noble temptation to see too much in everything. *Gilbert Keith Chesterton*

Silence is the unbearable repartee. *Gilbert Keith Chesterton*

You cannot live without lawyers, and certainly you cannot die without them. *Joseph Hodges Choate*

In those days he was wiser than he is now; he used frequently to take my advice. *Winston Churchill*

It saves a lot of trouble if, instead of having to earn money and save it, you can just go and borrow it. *Winston Churchill*

Men occasionally stumble over the truth, but most of them pick themselves up and hurry off as if nothing had happened. *Winston Churchill*

When you have no basis for an argument, abuse the plaintiff. *Marcus Tullius Cicero*

Middle age: When you begin to exchange your emotions for symptoms. *Irvin Shewsbury Cobb*

Men will wrangle for religion; write for it; fight for it; die for it; anything but live for it. *Charles Caleb Colton*

If you don't say anything, you won't be called on to repeat it. *Calvin Coolidge*

No civilized person ever goes to bed the same day he gets up. *Richard Harding Davis*

My idea of an agreeable person is a person who agrees with me. *Benjamin Disraeli*

Talk to a man about himself and he will listen for hours. *Benjamin Disraeli*

All generalizations are dangerous, even this one. *Alexandre Dumas*

If a man is wise, he gets rich, and if he gets rich, he gets foolish, or his wife does. *Finley Peter Dunne*

A lie with a purpose is one of the worst kind, and the most profitable. *Finley Peter Dunne*

One of the strangest things about life is that the poor, who need money the most, are the very ones that never have it. *Finley Peter Dunne*

The only good husbands stay bachelors; they're too considerate to get married. *Finley Peter Dunne*

When a man sits with a pretty girl for an hour, it seems like a minute. But let him sit on a hot stove for a minute—and it's longer than any hour. That's relativity. *Albert Einstein*

Fame is proof that the people are gullible. *Ralph Waldo Emerson*

Creditors have better memories than debtors. *Benjamin Franklin*

You've no idea what a poor opinion I have of myself, and how little I deserve it. *William Schwenck Gilbert*

It isn't so much what's on the table that matters, as what's on the chairs. *William Schwenck Gilbert*

I know only two tunes; one of them is "Yankee Doodle," and the other isn't. *Ulysses Simpson Grant*

Modesty: The gentle art of enhancing your charm by pretending not to be aware of it. *Oliver Herford*

Women give us solace, but if it were not for women we should never need solace. *Don Herold*

Genius is an infinite capacity for giving pains. *Don Herold*

A humorist is a man who feels bad but who feels good about it. *Don Herold*

Work is the greatest thing in the world, so we should always save some of it for tomorrow. *Don Herold*

It is a good thing that life is not as serious as it seems to a waiter. *Don Herold*

I wish I were either rich enough or poor enough to do a lot of things that are impossible in my present comfortable circumstances. *Don Herold*

One thing this country needs is a clearinghouse for coat hangers. *Don Herold*

Pretty much all the honest truth-telling there is in the world is done by children. *Oliver Wendell Holmes*

About the only thing on a farm that has an easy time is the dog. *Edgar Watson Howe*

No man would listen to you talk if he didn't know it was his turn next. *Edgar Watson Howe*

Genius may have its limitations, but stupidity is not thus handicapped. *Elbert Hubbard*

The path of civilization is paved with tin cans. *Elbert Hubbard*

The fellow that owns his own home is always just coming out of a hardware store. *Elbert Hubbard*

It makes no difference what it is, a woman will buy anything she thinks a store is losing money on. *Elbert Hubbard*

When a fellow says, "It ain't the money, but the principle of the thing," it's the money. *Elbert Hubbard*

Everything bows to success, even grammar. *Victor Hugo*

Playing Shakespeare is so tiring. You never get a chance to sit down unless you're a king. *Josephine Hull*

The only completely consistent people are the dead. *Aldous Huxley*

I like work; it fascinates me; I can sit and look at it for hours. *Jerome K. Jerome*

He was so benevolent, so merciful a man that he would have held an umbrella over a duck in a shower of rain. *Douglas Jerrold*

I hate mankind, for I think myself one of the best of them, and I know how bad I am. *Samuel Johnson*

They gave each other a smile with a future in it. *Ring Lardner*

In the misfortune of our best friends we find something which is not displeasing to us. *François de la Rochefoucauld*

We all have enough strength to bear the misfortunes of others. *François de la Rochefoucauld*

Many a man in love with a dimple makes the mistake of marrying the whole girl. *Stephen Leacock*

I've given up reading books; I find it takes my mind off myself. *Oscar Levant*

The first thing I do in the morning is brush my teeth and sharpen my tongue. *Oscar Levant*

Fishing is a delusion entirely surrounded by liars in old clothes. *Don Marquis*

I was not accustomed to flattery; I was like the Hoosier who loved gingerbread better than any man and got less of it. *Abraham Lincoln*

A politician is a person with whose politics you don't agree; if you agree with him he is a statesman. *David Lloyd George*

"Be yourself!" is about the worst advice you can give to some people. *Tom Masson*

Conscience: The inner voice which warns us that someone may be looking. *H. L. Mencken*

Don't talk about yourself; it will be done when you leave. *Addison Mizner*

A good listener is not only popular everywhere, but after a while he knows something. *Wilson Mizner*

Some of the greatest love affairs I've known have involved one actor—unassisted. *Wilson Mizner*

Be nice to people on your way up because you'll meet them on your way down. *Wilson Mizner*

There is nothing so consoling as to find that one's neighbor's troubles are at least as great as one's own. *George Moore*

By the time the youngest children have learned to keep the place tidy, the oldest grandchildren are on hand to tear it to pieces again. *Christopher Morley*

In the midst of life we are in debt. *Ethel Watts Mumford*

I'm living so far beyond my income that we may almost be said to be living apart. *Hector Hugh Munro*

An optimist is a fellow who believes a housefly is looking for a way to get out. *George Jean Nathan*

The desire to take medicine is perhaps the greatest feature which distinguishes man from animals. *William Osler*

This is the final test of a gentleman: his respect for those who can be of no possible service to him. *William Lyon Phelps*

In national affairs a million is only a drop in the budget. *Burton Rascoe*

Before I got married I had six theories about bringing up children; now I have six children and no theories. *Lord Rochester*

A radical is a man with both feet firmly planted in the air. *Franklin Delano Roosevelt*

A miser grows rich by seeming poor; an extravagant man grows poor by seeming rich. *William Shakespeare*

Few people think more than two or three times a year; I have made an international reputation for myself by thinking once or twice a week. *George Bernard Shaw*

If all economists were laid end to end, they would not reach a conclusion. *George Bernard Shaw*

I often quote myself; it adds spice to my conversation. *George Bernard Shaw*

He is indebted to his memory for his jests and to his imagination for his facts. *Richard Brinsley Sheridan*

Man is an animal that makes bargains; no other animal does this—no dog exchanges bones with another. *Adam Smith*

He has returned from Italy a greater bore than ever; he bores on architecture, painting, statuary, and music. *Sydney Smith*

He is remarkably well, considering that he has been remarkably well for so many years. *Sydney Smith*

Macaulay has occasional flashes of silence that make his conversation perfectly delightful. *Sydney Smith*

Jazz will endure just as long as people hear it through their feet instead of their brains. *John Philip Sousa*

Men tire themselves in pursuit of rest. *Laurence Sterne*

May you live all the days of your life. *Jonathan Swift*

She wears her clothes as if they were thrown on her with a pitchfork. *Jonathan Swift*

When a true genius appears in the world, you may know him by this sign, that the dunces are all in confederacy against him. *Jonathan Swift*

The boy gathers materials for a temple, and then when he is thirty concludes to build a woodshed. *Henry David Thoreau*

City life: Millions of people being lonesome together. *Henry David Thoreau*

Well, if I called the wrong number, why did you answer the phone? *James Thurber*

All you need in this life is ignorance and confidence, and then success is sure. *Mark Twain*

Names are not always what they seem. The common Welsh name Bzjxxllwcp is pronounced Jackson. *Mark Twain*

By trying we can easily learn to endure adversity—another man's, I mean. *Mark Twain*

I can live for two months on a good compliment. *Mark Twain*

I like criticism, but it must be my way. *Mark Twain*

It usually takes me more than three weeks to prepare a good impromptu speech. *Mark Twain*

There are two times in a man's life when he should not speculate: when he can't afford it, and when he can. *Mark Twain*

To be good is noble, but to teach others how to be good is nobler—and less trouble. *Mark Twain*

To cease smoking is the easiest thing I ever did; I ought to know because I've done it a thousand times. *Mark Twain*

Wagner's music is better than it sounds. *Mark Twain*

Money won't buy happiness, but it will pay the salaries of a large research staff to study the problem. *Bill Vaughan*

The art of government consists in taking as much money as possible from one class of citizens to give to the other. *Voltaire*

I know I am among civilized men because they are fighting so savagely. *Voltaire*

I am saddest when I sing; so are those who hear me; they are sadder even than I am. *Artemus Ward*

There is but one pleasure in life equal to that of being called on to make an after dinner speech, and that is not being called on to make one. *Charles Dudley Warner*

Arguments are to be avoided; they are always vulgar and often convincing. *Oscar Wilde*

A cynic is a man who knows the price of everything and the value of nothing. *Oscar Wilde*

78

Experience is simply the name we give our mistakes. *Oscar Wilde*

George Moore wrote brilliant English until he discovered grammar. *Oscar Wilde*

He knew the precise psychological moment when to say nothing. *Oscar Wilde*

He was always late on principle, his principle being that punctuality is the thief of time. *Oscar Wilde*

In America, the young are always ready to give to those who are older than themselves the full benefits of their inexperience. *Oscar Wilde*

The public is wonderfully tolerant—it forgives everything except genius. *Oscar Wilde*

To love oneself is the beginning of a lifelong romance. *Oscar Wilde*

When I was young I used to think that money was the most important thing in life; now that I am old, I know it is. *Oscar Wilde*

When people agree with me, I always feel that I must be wrong. *Oscar Wilde*

The butler entered the room, a solemn procession of one. *Pelham Grenville Wodehouse*

It was one of those parties where you cough twice before you speak and then decide not to say it after all. *Pelham Grenville Wodehouse*

If it keeps up, man will atrophy all his limbs but the push-button finger. *Frank Lloyd Wright*

9

Youth and Age

Good Question

A young boy was helping his grandfather dig potatoes. After a while the child began to tire. "Grandpa," he asked wearily, "what made you bury these things anyway?"

Regrets

During his 100th birthday interview, the salty centenarian told the reporter, "If I'd known I was going to live this long, I'd have taken better care of myself."

Life at 40

BLOND TO FELLOW WORKER: I hate to think of life at forty.
REDHEAD: Why? What happened then?

Middle age: When you can do everything you used to do—but not until tomorrow.

Middle age: The time of life when you can feel bad in the morning without having fun the night before.

She Was Right

A dirty little boy came in from playing out-of-doors and asked his mother, "Who am I?"
Guessing, his mother replied, "Are you Tarzan?"
The boy replied, "The lady down the street was sure right."
"About what?" asked the mother.
"She said I was so dirty my own mother wouldn't recognize me."

Achievements and Age

Many of the world's great achievements are the work of men and women in the later years of life. Socrates gave the world his wisest philosophy at seventy. Plato was only a student at fifty. He did his best teaching after sixty. Bacon was sixty before he wrote his greatest works. Phillips Brooks, one of the world's distinguished preachers, was a major figure at eighty-four. Gladstone was a leader in political and intellectual circles when he was eighty. Goethe finished his *Faust* at eighty-two. Victor Hugo wrote his *Les Miserables* at sixty-two. Jules Verne was writing with wonderful imagination at seventy. Noah Webster wrote his great dictionary at seventy.

"Age is a quality of mind," as unknown author once wrote. He continued:

> If you left your dreams behind,
> If hope is cold,
> If you no longer look ahead,
> If your ambitions' fires are dead—
> Then you are old.
> But if from life you take the best,
> And if in life you keep the jest,
> If love you hold;
> No matter how the years go by,
> No matter how the birthdays fly—
> Then you are not old.

Herbert V. Prochnow

Grandparents

Third-grader's definition of a grandmother: A very nice lady who makes good fudge and knits good sweaters and keeps your mom from hollering at you and your dad from hitting you.

Grandfather: Someone who when you want something you get it.

Free

A grandfather took his two grandsons to one of those Saturday special movies for children. After paying for their tickets, he asked the cashier the price for an adult. She replied: "If you can take it, it's free."

Move Over

A friend tells of an old gentleman he met on a train.

"Have you any grandchildren?" the old fellow asked.

"Yes," my friend said.

Then the fellow went to another passenger and said, "Have you any grandchildren?"

"Yes," was the reply.

So he went to another, "Have you any grandchildren?"

"No."

"Move over," said the old gentleman happily. "I want to tell you about my grandchildren."

That Should Do It

The young mother had used every wile to make her youngster eat his dinner, to no avail. In desperation she used her last weapon. "Eat it, dear," she cooed. "Pretend it's mud."

Difficult Problem

"I'm going crazy at home," confided Billy to a classmate in the second grade. "It's my parents. If I make noise, they spank me, and if I'm quiet, they take my temperature."

He Didn't

MOTHER: Just look at your clothes! I told you not to jump over that strip of newly oiled road.

SON: Well, I didn't, Mom.

Meant Well

A lady was entertaining her friend's small son.

"Are you sure you can cut your meat?" she asked, after watching his struggles.

"Oh, yes," he replied, without looking up from his plate. "We often have it this tough at home."

Good Answer

The Scouts were in camp. In an inspection the director found an umbrella neatly rolled inside the bedroll of a small Scout. As an umbrella was not listed as a necessary item, the director asked the boy to explain.

"Sir," answered the young man with a weary sigh, "did you ever have a mother?"

Two Choices

"When I was a kid, my mother always offered me two choices at dinner—take it or leave it." *Sam Levenson*

Hospital Definitions

FIRST LITTLE BOY IN HOSPITAL WARD: Are you medical or surgical?

SECOND LITTLE BOY: I don't know. How do you tell?

FIRST LITTLE BOY: Were you sick when you came here, or did they make you sick after you got here?

Age

I used to burn, but now I smoulder. That's how I learn I'm growing older. *Christopher Morley*

He Was Somebody

When King George VI was a lad (known as Albert), he and his older brother, Edward, stood with noses pressed against a window, watching a group of urchins having a snowball fight outside the palace. When their governess left the room, they slipped out to join the fight. Soon, a badly aimed snowball smashed a palace window, bringing a guard on the run. He dragged the snow-covered group off to the precinct sergeant, who bellowed at the first lad, "What's your name, boy?"

"My name is Edward, Prince of Wales," said the boy, standing haughtily at attention.

"Oh yes? And what's yours?" he asked the second in line.

"Albert, Duke of York."

"What a bunch!" growled the sergeant. "And who are you?"

The next lad hesitated; then, wiping his nose on his sleeve, he replied, "I'm going to stand wiv my buddies, guvnor—I'm the Archbishop of Canterbury."

The Aging of Children

A first-grader recently proved how "with it" children really are. He slipped on the stairs of his school and skinned his knee. His teacher hurried over to help him and said, "Remember, Timmy, big boys don't cry."

Tim replied, "I'm not gonna cry. I'm gonna sue."

Intelligent Boy

A little boy decked out in a space helmet cornered his dad and announced: "Put 'er thar, you ornery old horned toad, or I'll plug you with my six-shooter."

"Wait a minute, son," protested the father, "you're talking Western, not space."

"I," retorted the son disdainfully, "hail from West Mars."

Not Too Clean

Dick, aged 3, did not like soap and water. One day his mother was trying to reason with him. "Surely you want to be a clean little boy, don't you?"

"Yes," tearfully agreed Dick, "but can't you just dust me?"

Precocious Child

The fact-finding youngster faced his mother one day asking: "Didn't you tell me the stork brought me?"

"Why, yes, dear."

"And I weighed eight pounds?"

"Yes."

"Well, for your information," said the boy, "the stork hasn't the wing spread to carry an eight-pound load."

An Old Chinese Proverb Goes Like This

A little boy was standing by the river, when a man came along carrying a big basket. "Where are you going," asked the boy. To which the man replied, "I am going to drown the old man who is in the basket, for he can no longer keep up with us." The little boy said, "Be sure to bring back the basket, for one day we will need it for you."

Retirement

When Henry Ford, on his seventy-fifth birthday, was asked when he planned to retire, he exclaimed: "I haven't given a bit of thought to it! I'm going to stay around as long as I can be of any use; and I want to be of use as long as I stay around!"

Wisdom at Sixty

A wise old lady of eighty tells her friends, as they reach sixty: "You have spent sixty years in preparation for life; you will now begin to live. At sixty you have learned what is worthwhile. You have conquered the worst forms of foolishness, you have reached a balanced period of life, knowing good from evil; what is precious, what is worthless. Danger is past, the mind is peaceful, evil is forgiven, the affections are strong, envy is weak. It is the happy age.

Bedtime

If anything makes a child thirstier than going to bed, it's knowing his parents have gone to bed, too.

These Days

These days a child who knows the value of a dollar must be mighty discouraged.

Parents

After all is said and done, the most important part of a child's background at any time is the love and companionship of his parents. Children will leave their most precious toys or the most fascinating game for a romp with Mommy and Daddy. The best gift parents can give children is themselves. *Annie Laurie Von Tun*

Middle Age

Perhaps middle age is, or should be, a period of shedding shells: the shell of ambition, the shell of material accumulations and possessions, the shell of ego. Perhaps one can shed at this stage in life, as one sheds in beach living, one's pride, one's false ambitions, one's mask, one's armor. Was that armor not put on to protect one from the competitive world? If one ceases to compete, does one need it? Perhaps one can at last in middle age, if not earlier, be completely oneself. And what a liberation that would be. *Anne Morrow Lindbergh*

84

Ability Is Yours at Any Age

It is human frailty that prevents one generation from understanding and trusting another. A young man of twenty-five will go into business and surround himself with others of his own age or younger. Rarely will he employ men older. He thinks they are fossils.

As he ages, he continues to feel confidence and faith in his contemporaries. Whereas at twenty-five he thought men of that age had a monopoly on intelligence and resourcefulness, so at forty he turns to men of his own age for assistance. By the time he is sixty, he distrusts anyone under forty, except for routine work.

We need to remind ourselves occasionally that neither young nor old men necessarily know it all. Integrity, imagination, and executive ability may exist in full bloom at any age in life.

Playthings

It now costs more to amuse a child than it once did to educate his father.

At Christmas, what the kids would like is something that will separate the men from the toys.

Remember?

An alarm clock is a mechanical device to wake up people who have no children.

First-Things-a-Boy-Learns Dept.

One of the first things a boy learns with a chemistry set is that he isn't likely to get another one.

Love

Children need love, especially when they do not deserve it. *Harold S. Hulbert*

Living a Second Life

At about the age when many men begin to consider themselves crossing over to the shady side of life—the half-century mark—Sir Christopher Wren, who built magnificent St. Paul's Cathedral in London in the seventeenth century, was entering enthusiastically upon a new career in a new profession. After serving as professor of astronomy at Gresham College and Oxford, he turned architect.

In the forty-one years after his forty-eighth birthday this amazing man executed fifty-three churches and cathedrals, most of which still stand as monuments to his greatness. Like the man James Whitcomb Riley wrote of who had "lived to three-score and ten and had the hang of it now and could do it again," Sir Christopher discovered the secret of living a second life and doing another life's work. *Robert R. Updegraff*

Achievement

At sixty-three Dryden began the translation of the *Aeneid*. John Colby, brother-in-law of Daniel Webster, learned to read after he was eighty-four, that he might read the Bible. Robert Hall learned Italian when past sixty, that he might read Dante in the original. Noah Webster studied seventeen languages after he was fifty. Ludovico, at one hundred and fifteen, wrote the memoirs of his times. Cicero said well that men are like wine: age sours the bad, and improves the good. *Orrison Swett Marden*

Our Playthings Go

So Nature deals with us, and takes away
Our playthings one by one, and by the hand
Leads us to rest so gently, that we go
Scarce knowing if we wish to go or stay,
Being too full of sleep to understand
How far the unknown transcends the what we know.

Henry Wadsworth Longfellow

Test Yourself

You may be old at 40 and young at 80; but you are genuinely old at any age if:
You feel old;
You feel you have learned all there is to learn;
You find yourself saying, "I'm too old to do that;"
You feel tomorrow holds no promise;
You take no interest in the activities of youth;
You would rather talk than listen;
You long for the "good old days," feeling they were the best.

Minnesota State Medical Association

Happiness

I keep thinking of the wisdom of Aristotle when he affirmed that happiness cannot be achieved in less than a complete lifetime. This means that the last chapter is just as important as is any other. It is good to be young, and it is also good to be old. Life is lived best if it is lived in chapters, the point being to know in which chapter one is, and not to pine for what is not.
Elton Trueblood, American theologian

Happy Now

A little boy prayed: "Lord, if you can't make me a better boy, don't worry about it. I'm having a real good time as it is."

Did Well

"Mom," the little boy asked, "is the stork that brought me the same stork that brings ants, spiders and frogs?"

"Yes, dear," she answered.

"Then you didn't do so bad after all, did you?"

Letters to Santa

How many of the young folks who wrote letters to Santa Claus before Christmas, wrote him a thank-you letter after Christmas?

The Vanished Smack

As the poet said of juvenile delinquency, "Oh, for the smack of a vanished hand on the place where the smack ought to be."

Middle Age

When you bend over once to pick up two things, you are middle-aged.

His Father Knew

A boy was a witness in court, and the lawyer asked, "Did anyone tell you what to say in court?"

"Yes, sir," answered the boy.

"I thought so," exclaimed the lawyer. "Now you'll have to tell me who it was that told you."

"My father, sir."

"Your father," said the surprised lawyer. "And what did he tell you?"

"He said," the boy replied calmly, "the lawyers would try to get me tangled up, but if I stuck to the truth, I would be all right."

That's an Idea

WILLIE: Mamma, are you going to get the new coat you want from Santa Claus this Christmas?

MOTHER: I'm afraid not, my dear.

WILLIE: Have you tried throwing yourself on the floor and kicking with your feet and yelling like I do?

Careful

The mother questioned her young son before the arrival of the music teacher.

"Have you washed your hands carefully?"

"Yes, mother."

"And have you washed your face thoroughly?"

"Yes, mother."

"And did you wash behind your ears?"

"On her side I did, mother."

Memories Can Enrich

When a man reaches a certain age, he can begin to die by thinking he is getting old. An old man should think of what has gone before in his life. Life is a wonderful thing. Memories can enrich. *Pablo Casals (at age 90)*

Age and Accomplishment

Ah, nothing is too late,
Til the tired heart shall cease to palpitate.
Cato learned Greek at eighty; Sophocles
Wrote his grand Oedipus and Simonides
Bore off the prize of verse from his compeers,
When each had numbered more than fourscore years.
Chaucer, at Woodstock with the nightingales,
At sixty wrote the Canterbury Tales;
Goethe at Weimar, toiling to the last,
Completed Faust when eighty years were past.

Henry Wadsworth Longfellow

Contributions of Older Citizens

All of us know the tremendous contribution made by older citizens of the nation and of the world.

Winston Churchill, Prime Minister of Great Britain, at 81.

Clara Barton, president of the Red Cross at 83.

Robert Frost, writing poems after he turned 80.

Oliver Wendell Holmes, Justice of the Supreme Court until he was 91.

Connie Mack, managing the Philadelphia Athletics at 88.

Toscanini, conducting the National Broadcasting Company Orchestra at 87.

Frank Lloyd Write, designing the Guggenheim Museum at 86.

John Wesley, preaching at 88.

Congressman Lee H. Hamilton

The Contributions of Youth

The phenomenon we call the youth culture is not really so new. Through the ages, youth has made significant contributions to society. Consider the accomplishments of these "kids:"

Alfred Tennyson wrote his first volume at 18.

Alexander was a mere youth when he rolled back the Asiatic hordes that threatened to overwhelm European civilization.

Napoleon had conquered Italy at 25.

Byron and Raphael both died at 37, and Poe at 39, after writing their names among the world's immortals.

Newton made some of his greatest discoveries before he was 25.

Victor Hugo wrote a tragedy at 15.

Jesus Christ reshaped the world at 30.

Many of the world's greatest geniuses never saw 40.

Happy Childhood

A happy childhood is one of the best gifts that parents have it in their power to bestow. *Mary Cholmondeley*

Happy Children

If you make children happy now, you will make them happy twenty years hence by the memory of it. *Kate Douglas Wiggin*

Grandfather

Recently I watched a little girl swing lustily. Her hair flying, her eyes sparkling, her body going a bit higher at each turn of the swing. She was swinging to her heart's content—well, her little heart was not quite content with the mere motion of the swing. She kept calling, "Look, Diz. Look, Diz." (Perhaps I should explain that Diz is her name for her grandfather. . .) Half of the fun for the little girl was in having a friendly eye to watch her. *Ralph W. Sockman*

Obviously

Noticing some toadstools growing in the backyard for the first time, Louise went running to her mother and exclaimed, "Oh, mommy, frogs are going to move into our backyard! Their seats are there already!"

Raising Children

The trouble with modern homes is that too many parents use remote control in raising children.

Etiquette

Etiquette for a boy is saying, "No, thank you," when he wants more ice cream and cake.

Getting Old

If your back aches before you get out of bed, you are getting old.

If it takes you longer to rest than to get tired, you are getting old.

Quick!

Tact means to close your mouth before someone tells you to.

A Small Boy

A small boy is a pain in the neck when he is around, and a pain in the heart when he is not.

Child Psychology

"Handle this child carefully," the child specialist said to the mother.

"Remember, you're dealing with a sensitive, high-strung little stinker."

Staying Young

Whatever your years, there is in every being's heart the love of wonder, the undaunted challenge of events, and unfailing, childlike appetite for "what next," and the joy and game of life. You are as young as your faith, as old as your doubt; as young as your self-confidence, as old as your fear; as young as your hope, as old as your despair. In the central place of your heart, there is a recording chamber; so long as it receives messages of beauty, hope, cheer, and courage, so long you are young. *General Douglas MacArthur*

The Best Investment

In his book, *An Open Road*, Richard L. Evans writes: "A certain woman was heard to say as she observed a manly young man, 'I would give twenty years of my life to have such a son.' And the mother of the young man was heard to say, 'That's what I have given—twenty years of my life to have such a son.'

"But what better purpose would there be to take time for? Where is all the whirl of running around and splintering our lives into a thousand less meaningful interests and activities; where could we better take time? Where could we better invest for the future than in our families?"

The Most Important

The most important thing a father can do for his children is to love their mother. *Kirk Douglas*

The Best Is Yet to Be

"Grow old along with me—the best is yet to be." Vanderbilt at 80 added more than a hundred million to his fortune. Wordsworth earned the laureateship at 73. Thiers at 73 established the French Republic and became the first president. Verdi wrote "Falstaff" at 80. Gladstone became prime minister of England for the fourth time at 83. Stradivari made his first violin after 60. And Sir Walter Scott was $600,000 in debt at 55, but through his own efforts paid this amount in full, and built a lasting name for himself.

Not Only the Camel

Not only the camel, but Johnnie also could do without water for eight days if his mother would let him.

The Difference

A boy becomes a man when he walks around a puddle, not through it.

10

Work

What Happened?

BOSS: Nicholas, you should have been here at eight o'clock.
NICK: Why? What happened?

Thrifty Aunt

Joe the janitor had accumulated $50,000 and was going to retire. As was customary, the company gave a farewell dinner, and Joe was asked to say a few words.

"I owe my retirement in part to my thrifty habits," Joe said. "Even more, I owe it to the good judgment of my wife. But still more, I owe it to my aunt who died and left me $49,500."

Going into Debt

Nothing puts a family in debt as much as a small raise.

Always Agrees

"I never clash with my boss."
"No?"
"No, he goes his way and I go his."

Correct

Signs for desk-top baskets: "IN" "OUT" "STALLED"

Understood

To the girl who was applying for a job as typist, the employer said: "You claim you have plenty of speed and are good at spelling, but do you understand the importance of punctuation?"

"Oh, yes, indeed," she replied. "I always get to work on time."

Efficient Secretary

Secretary, handing letter to boss: "This one is marked 'Personal,' but it isn't really."

Experience

A secretary applying for a new job wrote under "Experience": "I'm familiar with all important phases of office procedures, including bowling and collection taking."

Without experience one gains no wisdom. *Chinese Proverb*

A Lot of Pipe

A plumber's apprentice was complaining to his boss about being pushed too hard on the job.

"Listen, son," said the old-timer, "when I was your age and first started plumbing, the boss laid the first two lengths of pipe to show us how. Then he turned on the water and we had to stay ahead of it."

Definitions

Patience: What you have when your boss makes the mistake.

Boss: A person you should never get smart with; you might be a guy he is able to part with.

Executive: One who never puts off until tomorrow what he can get someone else to do.

Honest

Albert is an excellent shipping clerk at the Jones Press. On his first day on the job, he found himself alone in the shipping room, when a professor telephoned with a long and complicated question. Albert listened patiently, and when at last the professor finished, he replied: "Guess I can't help you, Professor, because when I said 'Hello' I told you everything I know about this place."

Long Time No See

CUSTOMER: How long have you been working here?
WAITER: I've only been here a week.
CUSTOMER: Then you couldn't be the one who took my order!

Kept His Word

The Mayor of New York, the irrepressible Fiorello LaGuardia, was my first boss. A cardinal tenet of his management creed was that "Files are the curse of modern civilization." He delighted in relating a story about a young secretary he once hired right out of high school.

"I told her," he said, "if you can keep these files straight, I'll marry you." Then with a grin, he would add: "She did, so I married her!" *David Rockefeller*

Working Clothes

The late Prime Minister David Ben-Gurion of Israel disliked formal attire. In his office he wore a pair of slacks and a shirt open at the collar.

Once, at a diplomatic reception, he had to wear the traditional striped trousers and cutaway. Observing the raised eyebrows, he said apologetically, "Please forgive my appearance. These are my working clothes."

We Always Wondered Why

One reason computers can do more work than people is that they don't have to stop to answer the phone.

No Vacancy

When Eddie, the slow-moving clerk in a small store, was not in evidence one morning, a customer asked, "Where's Eddie? He ain't sick, is he?"

"Nope, Eddie ain't workin' here no more."

"That so?" said the customer. "Got anybody in mind for the vacancy?"

"Nope, Eddie didn't leave no vacancy."

Mistaken Identity

The new employee limped up to the foreman at the end of a long day of backbreaking work.

"Boss, are you sure you got my name right?" he asked.

"It's right here—you're Joe Simpson, aren't you?" the foreman replied.

"Yeah, that's it," moaned the fellow. "I was just checking—I thought maybe you had me down as Samson."

Makes a Difference

PERSONNEL DIRECTOR: And how many words can you type per minute?

WOULD-BE TYPIST: Big or little ones?

He Said, "QUIET"

Stenographer to office manager: "I've taken all the criticism of my work I'm going to take! How do you spell 'quit'?"

In Grandpa's Time

Even in Grandpa's time there was something to make you sleep. They called it work.

Not Qualified

BRICKLAYER: I'd like to work here, but there's no place to park my car.

FOREMAN: I guess you won't do. We hire only bricklayers with chauffeurs.

He Earned It

A Texan was having dinner with friends one evening when the conversation turned to talk about children.

"Some day when you're down our way," said the Texan, "I'd like to have you see my son's ranch. He's only sixteen but he's already got himself a magnificent spread, and he earned it all—every bit of it."

Someone asked how a sixteen-year-old managed to earn a big ranch and the Texan replied: "By hustling. That boy," he drawled, "got two A's and a B on his report card last semester."

That's Different

It was lunchtime and the new file clerk, already notorious for misplacing things in the files, was furiously opening and closing drawers.

"Come on now," said her supervisor, trying to be helpful. "Whatever you've lost can wait until after lunch."

"Not this time," she answered desperately. "It is my lunch."

The trouble with staying home from work is that you have to drink coffee on your own time.

The Boss

Just because nobody disagrees with you doesn't necessarily mean you are brilliant—maybe you're the boss.

The boss who put his picture on the clock was not dumb. It stopped clock-watching.

The difference between a junior and senior executive may be as much as forty pounds.

When We Fail to Praise

John Ruskin once said that when we fail to praise someone who deserves praise, two sad things happen: We run a chance of driving him from the right road for want of encouragement, and we deprive ourselves of one of the very happiest of our privileges—the privilege of rewarding labor that deserves a reward.

Hard Work

I believe in work, hard work, and long hours of work. Men do not break down from overwork, but from worry and dissipation. *Charles Evans Hughes*

Most men came farthest fastest when they worked the mostest.

A good traffic cop whistles at his work.

Not only is the horse just about extinct, but so are the people who work like one.

Time Off

A vacation should be just long enough for the boss to miss you, and not long enough for him to discover how well he can get along without you.

There is a difference between a man who does good for a salary and one who does good with his salary.

Loyalty

"I suppose," said the man to the boy applying for a job, "you have a host of activities of your own that will be a great deal more important than anything here. You are interested in ball games and . . ." The boy replied promptly, "Yes, sir, I like baseball first-rate; and I play it for all I'm worth. But when I am here, I'll be all here. I ain't big enough to divide." *Moody Monthly*

Big Business?

A business is too big when it takes a week for gossip to go from one end of the office to the other.

Hard to Explain

Said Hal to Pal, "I don't see how a watch can keep accurate time."
Said Pal to Hal, "Why not?"
Said Hal to Pal, "Well, time flies, but a watch only runs."

Definition

Conference: A meeting at which people talk about what they should be doing.

Discouraged

"You told me how good you were when I hired you two weeks ago," said a foreman to one of his men, "Now tell me all over again. I'm getting discouraged."

Good Reason

A man applying for a job was told that the firm was overstaffed. "Sure, but you could still hire me," he said. "The little bit of work I'd do would never be noticed."

Wages

A psychologist says the smallest things in life are the most essential, which describes our own bankroll.

There are people who figure they ought to have high wages on their first job, because it's harder work when you don't know anything about it.

A love of money may be the root of all evil, but it is also the root of a lot of hard work.

It is better to get bent from hard work than to get crooked trying to avoid it.

A union worker wrote home: "Having a wonderful time and a half."

Worst Job
Doing nothing is the most tiresome job in the world, because you can't quit and rest.

Grandpa may have had to work hard but he never had to clean a swimming pool.

Obvious
Three-fourths of Earth's surface is water and one-fourth is land. It's obvious that the Good Lord intended that man should spend three times as much time fishing as plowing.

Leisure
Those who are harping for and who wish for a 25- or 30-hour work week might do well to ponder that no civilization in history has ever been able to make use of a large amount of leisure profitably and still remain a great civilization. Perhaps we can do it, but a very intelligent appraisal and a very great dedication to service will be required of us. *General Alfred M. Gruenther*

Efficiency
He did nothing in particular, and did it very well. *W. S. Gilbert*

His Routine
Like so many literary greats, Charles Lamb was not suited for the daily routine of the office work he was forced to take in order to make ends meet. The office manager once said to him, "Mr. Lamb, it has been brought to my attention that you come very late to the office."

"Yes, sir," replied the writer, "but you must remember that I leave very early." *Coronet*

11

Making Progress

Should Look Well

Mrs. Murphy was at the wake of her husband. A friend came up to her and stood alongside the casket and said, "My, doesn't he look wonderful."

"Well," she said, "He ought to; he's been jogging three miles a day." *Thomas C. Morrill*

Faced a Problem

An engineer engaged in railroad construction in Central America explained to one of the persons living alongside the right-of-way the advantages the new road would bring him. Wanting to illustrate his point, he asked the person, "How long does it take to carry your produce to market by muleback?"

"Three days."

"Then," said the engineer, "you can understand the benefit that road will be to you. You will be able to take your produce to market and return home on the same day."

"Very good," the person agreed courteously. "But, señor, what shall I do with the other two days?"

Same Result

A hundred years ago there were no laundries or dry cleaners. People just tore off their own buttons.

One Exception

A TV repair service ad: "We can fix anything wrong with your TV except the lousy programs."

Always Sings

During my crusade in Scotland, I was staying at a hotel in Edinburgh. One morning I was delighted to hear the strains of "Onward Christian Soldiers" in the kitchen. I tiptoed to the door to give the cook my compliments.

"Oh," said the Scot, "I always sing that hymn when I boil eggs. Three verses for soft, and five for hard-boiled." *Wit of Billy Graham*

Be Careful

An Army major called to a Navy enlisted man from across the room. "Sergeant!" There was no answer.

"Sergeant!" repeated the major, with still no answer from the Navy man.

Vexed at being ignored, the major walked over to where the man was sitting and tapped him on the shoulder. "Sergeant," he said, "I called you."

The Navy man looked up, and, with a touch of indignation, stated, "I'm not a sergeant. I'm a first-class petty officer in the U.S. Navy!"

"Well, if you were in the Army, you'd be a sergeant!" was the reply.

"No, sir," said the sailor. "If I was in the Army, I'd be a major!" *True*

Going Forward

J. Duncan Spaeth, the late Shakespearian scholar and crew coach, was fond of saying that he liked rowing as a sport because he would rather be a man who was looking backward and going forward than one who was looking forward and going backward. That makes sense. It is not enough merely to look ahead; we must also move ahead. *William H. Hudnut, Jr.*

Put It Off

Always put off until tomorrow what you are going to make a mess of today.

The Brain

Dr. Charles Mayo once said: "It's the brain that counts. An old man can get along with a wooden leg but not with a wooden head."

Counting Your Money

Sometimes it isn't until you count your money that you realize just how carefree your vacation really was.

They say you can't take it with you, but have you ever tried to travel very far without it?

Acquainted Now

On Fifth Avenue a man and woman, coming in opposite directions, jockeyed to the right, then to the left, several times in an effort to pass each other. Finally the way cleared and the man politely tipped his hat and said, "Well, good-bye, it's been fun knowing you!"

Either

"Which way for the train to Boston?" inquired an old lady. "Walk straight ahead," said the gateman, "turn to the left and you'll be right."

"Young man, don't be facetious with me."

"All right, Madam, turn to the right and you'll be left!"

A Natural Leader

In the American advance during the last days of World War I, a sergeant ordered a private to go into a dugout and disperse any enemies who happened to be there.

The private swallowed his Adam's apple, and then said, huskily, "Sergeant, if you see three or four men come running out of that hole, don't shoot the first one!"

Just Desserts

"Look here, waiter, is this peach or apple pie?"

"What does it taste like?"

"It tastes like glue."

"Well, then it must be apple pie, because our peach pie tastes like putty."

Popular Songs

Whatever isn't worth saying will be made into a popular song.

The old hit songs are best because no one sings them any longer.

Balanced Thinking

Place a four-inch plank across the floor of a room and any man can walk along it without any difficulty whatever. But place the same plank above the street from the top of the town's two highest buildings, and hardly a man can be found who can walk across it. What is the difference? The same plank, the same muscles, the same mind, the same will. The difference is that when the plank is on the floor, we are thinking only of walking across; and when the plank is suspended in the air, we are thinking more about falling.

What is wrong with a man whose life is full of little fears and whose mind is beset by worries? He is thinking about falling off and not about staying on. You cannot make progress toward your goal while you look at the ditch into which you fear you may fall. You cannot go forward with the full sweep of your personality in constructive, progressive thinking and development while in the whirlpool of negative thinking. *Sunshine Magazine*

Showery Appreciation

The businessman was annoyed, but he tried to hide his feelings. "I'm glad you like it, madam," he replied, "but why did you have to call me in the middle of the night to tell me?"

"Because," answered the housewife sweetly, "your truck just delivered it."

Getting in Shape
The second day of a diet is easier because by that time you are off it.

Most persons not only keep their youthful figures as they grow older: they double them.

Passing the Finish Line
You can win $5,000 at the race track—if you're the horse.

To get to the promised land, you generally have to go through the wilderness.

Senior citizens are unwilling dropouts from the school of hard knocks.

Not So Fast
FORTUNE TELLER: I charge ten dollars for two questions.
CLIENT: Isn't that rather high?
FORTUNE TELLER: Yes. Now what is your second question?

Indian Corn
Visiting an Indian reservation, a tourist asked the Chief about the size of his family and was amazed when the Chief said he had fourteen kids. "Well," said the tourist, "with a family that large, don't you have endless squabbles, fights and arguments?"
"Oh, no," the Chief replied. "We're just one big Hopi family."

Good As New
"That is a good-looking hat you are wearing."
"Yes, I bought if five years ago, had it cleaned three times, changed it twice in restaurants, and it's still as good as new."

In and Out
Everyone can give pleasure in some way. One person may do it by coming into a room, and another by going out.

A first-class hotel is one in which you pay $10 extra to get the morning paper slipped under your door.

The salt business must be prospering—people are taking things more now with a grain of salt.

When the young man said he would die for her, the cynical young lady wanted to know how soon.

Odd . . .

It's difficult to understand why other people do not profit by their mistakes.

Frog

Abraham Lincoln had the light touch which is a saving ingredient in any leader. Do you remember the account that Carl Sandburg relates as one of his favorite Lincoln stories? Lincoln told of a frog that was mired in a deep, muddy wagon track. His frog friends came and did everything they knew to encourage him to get out. Try as he would, he couldn't. Finally in despair, the frogs left. The next day they found the frog by the pond, chipper, joyful and real pleased with himself. They said, "We thought you couldn't get out of that rut." He replied, "I couldn't, but a wagon was coming and I had to." *Robert J. Lamont*

Naturally

A Londoner who got on a bus in Chelsea recently found himself the only white man among a dozen Africans on top.

The conductress came up to take his fare. She said: "Dr. Livingstone, I presume." *Peter Peterborough, Daily Telegraph, London*

No Cure

"Congratulations," said the psychiatrist to his patient. "You're cured."
"Some cure! Before, I was Julius Caesar. Now I'm a nobody."

The Bearer of Good News

It is said that ancient kings used to kill the bearer of bad news. We no longer follow that practice. Today it is the bearer of good news who is in danger. Of course, he is not in danger of death, but he is in danger of being considered shallow, dishonest or hardhearted. In today's world, if you can look about you and see that things are pretty good, you're not fit to be an editorial writer for *The New York Times*, my son. *Herbert Stein, Former Chairman, Council of Economic Advisers to the President*

A Tip

To have good luck fishing you have to get there yesterday when the fish were biting.

It takes 50 years to grow a great forest and then some chump drops a lighted match.

Wonder Drug

A wonder drug is a medicine that makes you wonder whether you can afford to get sick these days.

Weather

There are times when we understand what the weatherman means by the "mean" temperature.

Architecture

Novelty is mistaken for progress. Of steel and glass we have aplenty; but what of the imaginative and creative powers which makes these glittering materials structures responsible to the needs of the human individual? What of real sun, real air, real leisure? *Frank Lloyd Wright*

Civilization

Look back along the endless corridors of time and you will see that four things have built civilization: the spirit of religion, the spirit of creative art, the spirit of research, and the spirit of business enterprise. *Dr. Neil Carothers*

Spending

The advantage of keeping family accounts is clear. If you do not keep them you are uneasily aware of the fact that you are spending more than you are earning. If you do keep them, you know it. *Robert Benchley*

Being Contented

It's easy to be contented with what you have, but not with what you don't have.

Too Late

All things come to those who wait, but when they come they're out-of-date.

Worth Thinking About

Joy in one's lot is illustrated in a charming story told by William L. Stidger. One of his students was walking down a steep hill in Boston one day shortly after a snowfall and saw a youngster skiing with one ski. He stopped beside the boy and said, "Son, don't you know you are supposed to have two skis?" The lad looked up with a happy grin and replied, "I know I ought to have two, but I ain't got 'em. But, mister, you can have a lot of fun with one ski if you ain't got two." *Robert I. Kahn*

The New Year

Were it not for the observance of New Year, the passing of time might be monotonous and meaningless. We might watch the endless pattern of days and nights without fully realizing that time, like money, must be wisely spent, else it is wasted. That is why we need the New Year—to remind us that precious time has been spent or wasted, and even more valuable time is ours to use or to idle away.

Second Fiddle

A friend once asked a famous conductor of a great symphony orchestra which instrument in the orchestra he considered the most difficult to play. The conductor thought a moment, and then he said, "Second fiddle. I can get plenty of first violinists. But to find one who can play second fiddle with enthusiasm—that's the problem. And if we have no second fiddle, we have no harmony!"

Not Very Big

They gave all seniors a letter, and I can remember my high school coach's introduction of me to this day. As I came past that platform to get the letter, he said, "You take that Bob Delvaney. He is not very big, but he sure is slow." *As told by Robert Delvaney, Athletic Director, University of Nebraska*

Don't Let On

Intelligence is very much like money—if you don't let on how little you've got, people will treat you as though you had a lot.

Aesthetics

A curve may be more beautiful than a straight line, but not when it's a fast single over second base.

Popular Opinion

Popular opinion is the highest expression of man's intellect when it agrees with us, but it is mass ignorance when it disagrees with our views.

Time

No day is ever busier than tomorrow.

This is the time of the year when the person who was going to raise all his own vegetables is buying canned goods on sale.

We'll Remember

A gag at the Pentagon has it that one of the next astronauts to go up asked one of the first astronauts if he had any advice.

The first astronaut nodded thoughtfully and replied, "The whole secret is . . . don't look down." *Don MacLean*

12

School Days

Qualified
Sign on the door of a college basketball coach's office: "I'm busy but if you can see over the transom, come in."

Take Your Choice
Old teachers never die, they just lose their principals.
Old principals never die, they just lose their faculties.

Hard Job
Willy was sobbing bitterly. Between sobs, he told the teacher: "I don't like school, and I have to stay here until I am 16." "Don't let that worry you," consoled the teacher. "I have to stay here until I'm 65."

Advantage
Overheard at a teachers' meeting: "I prefer to teach in an elementary school. I know I'll have a place to park my car."

Expects Too Much
One professor always introduces his course on Shakespeare with these words:
"In this class, ladies and gentlemen, you will meet with some earthy four-letter words regarded as not quite proper in mixed groups. One of those words you must learn to accept and live with without embarrassment. I refer to the good old Anglo-Saxon term w-o-r-k." *E. H. Butler*

Study
If you neglect study when you are young, what of your old age? *Chinese Proverb*

The Novel
American novel—a story in which two people want each other from the beginning, but don't get each other until the end of the book.

French novel—a story in which two people get together right at the beginning, but from then on until the end of the book they don't want each other any more.

Russian novel—a story in which two people don't want each other or get each other—and for the next 800 pages they brood about it. *Novelist Erich Maria Remarque*

Nathan Hale's Comet?

A schoolboy turned in the following history essay: "It was Nathan Haley who said, 'I regret that I have but one life to give for my country.' This has come to be known as Haley's comment."

Sounds Reasonable

Two boys were talking about their respective dogs. "I can't figure it out," complained one. "How is it that you can teach your dog all those tricks and I can't teach my dog anything at all?"

"Well," said the other boy, "to begin with, you gotta know more than your dog."

Answer This Question

It was a bright spring morning and four high school boys decided to skip classes. Arriving after lunch, they explained to the teacher that their car had a flat tire along the way. To their relief, the teacher smiled understandingly and said: "You boys missed a test this morning. Please take your seats apart from one another and get out your paper and pencil."

When the boys were seated, she continued, "Answer this question: Which tire was flat?"

A Little Learning

The first time that a schoolboy realizes that a little learning is a dangerous thing is when he brings home a poor report card. *Mark Twain*

Good Review

A student in Mrs. Ada Kirk's ninth grade English class at the Cuero (Texas) High School ended a recent book report with this perceptive appraisal: "I think the author was a pretty good writer not to make the book no duller than it was." *John Scanlon, Saturday Review*

Who Are You?

There was a young lady waiting with her two children at one of the commuter stations on the Chicago Rapid Transit for her husband to return from the day's work. As the train pulled into the station the first person off the train was a professor, a very distinguished professor from Northwestern University. And he looked the part of a professor. He had a long, flowing, white mane, and carried a tightly rolled black umbrella, and all the other proper accouterments of a professor.

As he got off the train he spotted this young lady, and he walked right up to her, pointed at her, and said, "Joyce Smith, Philosophy 302; Spring semester, 1970; row five, seat twenty-two. Right?"

And she said, "That's right, but who are you?" *Dr. John E. Corbally, Jr., President, University of Illinois*

Behind the News

"The rain is really coming down. Reminds me of the Great Flood."

"The what?"

"The Great Flood . . . Noah . . . the Ark."

"I wouldn't know about that. I haven't had the TV on in four or five days."

Not Too Smart

A motorist was driving in the country when suddenly his car stopped. He got out and was checking the spark plugs when an old horse trotted up the road.

The horse said, "Better check the gas line," and trotted on.

The motorist was so frightened that he ran to the nearest farmhouse and told the farmer what had happened.

"Was it an old horse with a flopping ear?" inquired the farmer.

"Yes! Yes!" cried the frightened man.

"Well, don't pay any attention to him," replied the farmer. "He doesn't know much about cars."

Adult Education

With all the emphasis on methods of adult education, we still maintain there is nothing better than children.

He Asked for It

FIRST STUDENT: You look all broken up. What's wrong?
SECOND STUDENT: I wrote home for money for a study lamp.
FIRST STUDENT: So what?
SECOND STUDENT: They sent the lamp.

It Didn't Help Him

A fifteen-year-old was discussing her report card. "No wonder Jean always gets an A in French," she observed. "Her father and mother speak French at the table."

"If that's the case," her boyfriend said, "I ought to get an A in geometry. My parents talk in circles!"

Simple

TEACHER: If you had seven pieces of candy and I asked for four of them, how many would you have left?

FIRST-GRADER (*matter-of-factly*): Seven.

Correct

TEACHER: What is the Alamo?

BRIGHT BOY: That's pie with ice cream on it.

Hire Education

A recent survey of college students revealed the following vocational careers they hoped to pursue: Hosale saleman, technction, physist, piolet, archact, augriculter, teecher, writter, psyciartist, lybrarian, and adminastor.

Some students selected: engeniering, engenearing, or engeening. Others preferred: bussinuss, denestry, episcopailan, leberal, and schology. Naturally, some wrote undesided.

Education

I was a modest, good-humored boy. It is Oxford that has made me insufferable. *Sir Max Beerbohm*

Self-Confidence

A Balliol education gives a man a tranquil sense of effortless superiority. *The late Lord Oxford and Asquith*

Anti-Climax

Waggish non-Yale men never seem to weary of calling "For God, for Country and for Yale," the outstanding anti-climax in the English language. *Time*

Only Child

CHILD: My teacher asked me if I had any brothers or sisters.

MOTHER: How nice of her to take an interest in you!

CHILD: Yes, and when I told her I was an only child, she said, 'Thank goodness!'

Progress?

Father to son, looking at his report card: "Your grades don't promise much of a future, but your conduct marks indicate that you've already had quite a past!"

Any More Outstanding Results?

The chemistry teacher was giving his class a verbal quiz. "What," he asked, "is the most outstanding result of the use of chemistry in the past five hundred years?"

"Blondes!" came the quick reply.

Smart Alec

TEACHER: What is the half of eight, Frank?

FRANK: Which way, teacher?

TEACHER: What do you mean?

FRANK: On top or sideways?

TEACHER: What difference does it make?

FRANK: Well, the top half of eight is zero, but the half of eight sideways is three.

From Texas

A Texas lad rushed home from kindergarten and insisted that his mother buy him a set of pistols, holster, and gun belt.

"Why, whatever for, dear?" mother asked. "You're not going to tell me you need them for school?"

"Yes, I do," he asserted. "Teacher said tomorrow she's going to teach us to draw."

Easier

An ironworker was nonchalantly walking the beams high above the street on a new skyscraper, while the pneumatic hammers made a nerve-jangling racket, and the compressor below shook the whole steel structure. When he came down, a man who had been watching him, tapped his shoulder. "I was amazed at your calmness up there. How did you happen to go to work on a job like this?"

"Well," said the other, "I used to drive a school bus, but my nerves gave out."

Great Teacher

Bill Lehr of New Castle (Indiana) tells of one pupil's definition of an excellent teacher in the system: "Even when I don't fully understand a thing she's talking about, she makes it interesting." *Marie Fraser, Indiana Teacher*

He Knew

The boy brought home his examination paper and his father was surprised when he read his son's answer to the following question: "What are the last two lines to the first verse of 'The Star-Spangled Banner'?"

His son's answer read: "And the home of the brave. Play ball."

That Would Have Helped

Rejected by the college of his choice, the banker's son angrily accosted his father. "If you really cared for me, you'd have pulled some wires!"

"I know," replied the parent sadly. "The TV, the hi-fi, and the telephone would have done for a start."

That Helped

A father was telling a friend how he had cured his son's habit of being late to school. "All I did," he explained, "was to buy him a car of his own."

"Just how did that stop him from being late?" inquired the friend.

"Why, he had to get there early to find a parking place."

They Knew the Real Answer

A teacher had just given a primary grade class a science lesson on magnet. In the follow-up test, one question read: "My name starts with 'M,' has six letters, and I pick up things. What am I?" She was a bit surprised to find that half the class answered the question with the word "Mother."

He Has a Problem

"I sure wish you'd let me take my bath in the morning instead of at night," a first-grader said to his mother one evening. "Our teacher always asks us whether or not we've had a bath today, and I haven't been able to say yes all year."

Keeps Him Kind

A five-year-old boy had been having trouble at the hands of another kindergarten youngster. One day, on his return from school, he remarked to his mother: "Johnny isn't nasty to me now; every time I see him, I hit him to keep him kind."

Correct

"An abstract noun," the teacher said, "is something you can think of, but you can't touch it. Can you give me an example of one?"

"Sure," a teenage boy replied. "My father's new car."

Trying to Please

"I hope," said the teacher, "that all you children had a pleasant holiday and have returned with more sense than when you left."

One eager-to-please boy replied, "Same to you, Miss Andrews."

He Was Good

MOTHER: Well, son, were you a good boy in school today?

SON: Sure, Mom—how much trouble can you get into while you stand in a corner all day?

School

First day of school! On that memorable morning in September, man takes his first giant step out into the world. It's a lonely step, even though parents hover as watchful as birds the day their nestlings leave. For now a fellow must create his own identity, solve his own problems. Will the others like me? How about the teacher? Can I ever learn to cut, to color, to read? But as the hours pass, fears give way to joys: new friends of his own making, the shine of gold stars and the eternal wonder of learning. *Richard C. Davis, Farm Journal*

It Helps

Education is what helps a lot of folks get along without intelligence.

Our Greatest Asset

It isn't quite true that youth is our country's greatest asset. Wisdom is our greatest asset, and wisdom is gained through experience in schools. Our youth must get their training and experience in the high schools and colleges today. *Walter H. Judd*

Opinion

Nothing contributes more to peace of mind than to have no opinions whatever. *G. C. Lichtenberg*

A Scholar

We live in a time of such rapid change and growth of knowledge that only he who is in a fundamental sense a scholar—that is, a person who continues to learn and inquire—can hope to keep pace, let alone play the role of guide. *Nathan Pusey, Former President of Harvard University*

Fools or Wise Men

Thales, philosopher of Greece, Ptolemy, astronomer of Alexandria, and perhaps others, believed that the earth was round. But the rest of the learned men, and the unlearned masses, thought the earth was a more or less flat disk. Not until Magellan sailed around it was the error of centuries exploded.

Aristotle taught that if a one-pound ball and a five-pound ball of the same size were dropped at the same time from the same height, the five-pound ball would fall five times as fast as the one-pound ball. For nearly two thousand years that proposition was accepted as a fact. The great Aristotle had said it—and it did sound "reasonable!" Then along came Galileo. He questioned it. He invited the Aristotelian scholars of his day to meet him—not to argue, but to ascend the tower of Pisa with him. There and then the experiment was tried—for the first time by anyone. Aristotle's theorem instantly became a dead duck. The two balls hit the ground at the same time.

The fool argues—the wise man experiments. There is no telling what transformation might be worked in human life—for its betterment and the promotion of happiness—if we argued less and experimented more. *Sunshine Magazine*

Some Drink
Some students drink at the fountain of knowledge; others just gargle.

Beginning to Get the Idea
Sixty years ago I knew everything; now I know nothing; education is a progressive discovery of our own ignorance. *Will Durant*

Firsthand Knowledge
You can get a lot of firsthand knowledge from a second hand TV set or automobile.

The Final Test
The final test of science is not whether it adds to our comfort, knowledge and power, but whether it adds to our dignity as men, our sense of truth. *David Sarnoff*

Boners
A momentum is what you give a person when he is leaving.

The line opposite the right angle in a right-angled triangle is called the hippopotamus.

Do You Need One?
An American tourist was greatly impressed by the Colosseum in Rome, Italy.

"Boy, what a nifty stadium," he remarked admiringly. "Where's the college?"

Amateur
An amateur athlete is one who doesn't take anything unless it's called a scholarship.

Yeah!
FATHER: Well, Willie, what did you learn at school today?

WILLIE *(proudly)*: I learned to say "Yes sir" and "No sir," and "Yes ma'am" and "No ma'am."

FATHER: You did?

WILLIE: Yeah!

Jimmy Knew His Animals
"Jimmy, name some animals peculiar to the Arctic region."

"Lions, tigers, elephants."

"Do you mean to say you think you would find these animals in the Arctic zone?"

"No, ma'am. It would be peculiar if they were found there."

His Reason

Little Eddie was almost through his nightly prayer. "Bless my papa, bless my mamma, bless Aunt Jenny, and please make St. Louis the capital of Missouri. Amen," he concluded.

"Why, darling!" exclaimed his mother, deeply shocked. "Why on earth did you say such a thing?"

"Because," said Eddie, "that's what I put on my examination paper."

Wonderful Lines

INSTRUCTOR: Whatever made you write a thing like that?

STUDENT: It's Shakespeare.

INSTRUCTOR: Beautiful lines, aren't they?

Bad Cold

TEACHER: Johnny, give me a sentence with the word "sphere" in it.

JOHNNY: I have a sphere cold.

Correct

PROFESSOR: Name two pronouns.

STUDENT: Who? Me?

Definition

University: An institution that has room for 2,000 in its classrooms and 50,000 in its stadium.

He Got to Stay After School

TEACHER: Johnny, make a sentence with the words "effervescent" and "fiddlestick."

JOHNNY: Effervescent long enough covers on the bed, your fiddlestick out.

Now She Has

"Do you know that Teacher has never seen a horse in her life?" exclaimed little Maisie excitedly.

"What makes you think that?" asked Mother.

"Well," said Maisie, "Teacher told us to draw something, and I drew a picture of a horse—and she didn't know what it was!"

Warning

Jimmie came into the schoolroom one morning, plainly excited. "Yes,

Jimmie, what is it?'' asked the teacher.

"I don't want to scare you," said Jimmie, hesitatingly, "but my dad said if I didn't get better grades, someone is due for a lickin'.''

Getting Educated

An educated man may earn more, but it takes him about twenty years after graduating to get educated.

Naturally

FRESHIE: I can't find "airplane" in the dictionary.

SOPHO: Look on the flyleaf.

Hard to Answer

The boy who didn't like to go to school did some calculating with very astonishing results. The more you study, he said, the more you know. The more you know, the more you forget. The more you forget, the less you know. The less you know, the less you forget. The less you forget, the more you know. So what's the use of going to school?

Next Question

"Johnny," said the teacher, "how many seasons are there?"

And Johnny answered promptly. "Two, baseball and football."

Is That Clear?

The instructor said, "When we speak of the Seven Seas, let's be specific."

"Okay, Prof," replied the fresh frosh, "you be specific and I'll be Atlantic."

Battle

TEACHER: In which of his battles was King Gustavus Adolphus of Sweden slain?

PUPIL: I guess it was the last one.

Next Question

"Can anyone tell me the meaning of the word 'collision'?"

No answer.

"Well, when two things come together unexpectedly, that is a collision. Now can anyone give me an example?"

Johnny: "Twins."

Dog's Tales

"Some plants," said the teacher, "have the prefix *dog*. For instance, there is the dogrose, the dogwood, the dogviolet. Now name another plant prefixed by *dog*."

"I can," shouted a little redhead from the back row, "collie flower."

He Knew Five

TEACHER: How many zones has the Earth?
JOHNNY: Five.
TEACHER: Correct. Name them.
JOHNNY: Temperate zone, intemperate, mail, no parking, and O.

Correct

TEACHER: What does the word velocity mean?
SMALL BOY: Velocity? Why, velocity is the thing a feller lets go of a bee with.

Idea

Let the other fellow talk a little once in a while. You can't learn much by listening only to yourself.

Democracy

You can't tell a millionaire's son from a billionaire's. *Vance Packard, on democracy of preparatory schools*

College Education

Hanging around until you've caught on. *Robert Frost, defining a college education*

13

A Matter of Life & Death

No Complaints

During World War II Richard Wynn, on flight duty with the 8th Air Force in Europe, was shot down and captured by the Germans. After a year as prisoner of war, he escaped and made his way back to his bomber group in England. One of his first acts there was to hunt up the corporal on duty in the parachute building.

"Corporal," he said, "a year ago I had occasion to use one of the parachutes that your men had packed and I want you to know how delighted I was to find it in perfect working order. I give you my deepest compliments and appreciation."

"You know, Lieutenant, funny thing," the corporal replied. "In this work we never get any complaints."

Safety First

In tender, loving memory of Jasper Ewing Drakes—he had a sweet abiding faith in other people's brakes.

I Like Autumn

I like spring, but it is too young. I like summer, but it is too proud. So I like best of all, autumn, because its tone is mellower, its colors richer, and it is tinged a little with sorrow. Its golden richness speaks not of the innocence of spring, nor of the power of summer, but of the mellowness and kindly wisdom of approaching age. It knows the limitations of life and is content. *Lin Yutang*

Nothing

At birth we bring nothing; at death we take nothing. *Chinese Proverb*

The Meaning of Life

A man has made at least a start on discovering the meaning of human life when he plants shade trees under which he knows full well he will never sit. *Elton Trueblood*

Pythagoras used to say life resembles the Olympic Games: a few men strain their muscles to carry off a prize; others bring trinkets to sell to the crowd for a profit; and some there are (and not the worst) who seek no further advantage than to look at the show and see how and why everything is done. *Michel de Montaigne*

Duty

It is seldom very hard to do one's duty when one knows what it is, but it is often exceedingly difficult to find this out. *Samuel Butler*

Facts

Oh, don't tell me of facts—I never believe facts: you know Canning said nothing was so fallacious as facts, except figures. *Sydney Smith*

Futility

He has spent all his life in letting down empty buckets into empty wells, and he is frittering away his age in trying to draw them up again. *Sydney Smith*

Life's Heaviest Burden

An old man was approached by a young one, who said: "You are old and wise. Tell me, what is life's heaviest burden?" And the old man answered sadly, "To have no burden to carry."

Habit

It seems, in fact, as though the second half of a man's life is made up of nothing but the habits he has accumulated during the first half. *Feodor Dostoevski*

Today

Live today to the fullest! Remember it's the first day of the rest of your life.

Do It Now

If you would do a kindness, it is not wise to wait. You never know how quickly it's going to be too late.

It seems we have so little time to do the kindly things, before we realize the truth—we find that time has wings. We plan to give a word of cheer to one who needs a friend; we plan to see someone who's ill who may be near the end.

And there's a letter we should write to someone who is sad; our words may be just what they need to cheer and make them glad. It's easy to procrastinate and leave such tasks undone; but such a course will bring regrets when life's short race is run.

There is a cure for all these ills—just three words tell us how. To bring a speedy, perfect cure, they're simply: "Do it now!" *LeTourneau "Now"*

The Shadow of Reality

Why should we live with such hurry and waste of life? . . . When we are unhurried and wise, we perceive that only great and worthy things have any permanent and absolute existence, that petty fears and petty pleasures are but the shadow of the reality. *Henry David Thoreau*

Our Lives Are Albums

Our lives are albums written through
With good or ill, with false or true;
And as the blessed angels turn
The pages of our years,
God grant they read the good with smiles,
And blot the ill with tears!

John Greenleaf Whittier

Secret Sorrows

Believe me, every man has his secret sorrows, which the world knows not; and oftentimes we call a man cold when he is only sad. *Henry Wadsworth Longfellow*

Do Your Best

You better live your best and act your best and think your best today; for today is the sure preparation for tomorrow and all the other tomorrows that follow. *Harriet Martineau*

Life

Life, for most of us, is a continuous process of getting used to things we hadn't expected.

A Simple Life

We Japanese enjoy the small pleasures, not extravagance. I believe a man should have a simple life style—even if he can afford more. *Masaru Ibuka, chairman of Sony Corporation*

Cluttering Life

It is not merely the trivial which clutters our lives but the important as well. *Anne Morrow Lindbergh*

Things You Can't Recall

There are four things that cannot be recalled: an arrow that has left the bow; an opportunity that was neglected; a word that has been spoken; and a life that has been lived. And if one could be recalled, how would you change it? *Persian Proverb*

We Exist for Others

How extraordinary is the situation of us mortals. Each of us is here for a brief sojourn; for what purposes he knows not though he sometimes thinks he senses it. But without going deeper than our daily life, it is plain that we exist for our fellow-men—in the first place, for those upon whose smiles and welfare our happiness depends, and next for all those unknown to us personally, but to whose destinies we are bound by the tie of sympathy. A hundred times every day I remind myself that my inner and outer life depend on the labors of other men, living and dead, and that I must exert myself in order to give in the measure as I have received and am still receiving. *Albert Einstein*

Begin with Yourself

There's only one corner of the universe you can be certain of improving, and that's your own self. So you have to begin there, not outside, not on other people. That comes afterwards, when you've worked on your own corner. You've got to be good before you can do good—or at any rate do good without doing harm at the same time. Helping with one hand—and hurting with the other—that's what the ordinary reformer does. *Aldous Huxley*

Everybody thinks of changing humanity and nobody thinks of changing himself. *Tolstoy*

Conclusions

The American historian, Charles Beard, when asked to summarize briefly his conclusions based on a lifetime of historical research, gave us these pithy comments.

1. When it is dark, you can see the stars.
2. The bee that steals honey from the flower also fertilizes the flower.
3. He whom God would destroy he first makes mad.
4. The mill of God grinds slow but it grinds exceeding fine.

The Honorable Walter Dinsdale,
Member of Canadian Parliament

God asks no man whether he will accept life. That is not the choice. You must take it. The only choice is how. *Henry Ward Beecher*

Adversity

There is something about dark times that may actually lead to more profound thought on the central questions. It is possible for men to be more clear-eyed in disaster than they are in prosperity. It is surely no accident that the noblest literature of the ancient Hebrews was produced during the Babylonian captivity and that the noblest words ever uttered in America came in the darkness of the Civil War. *Elton Trueblood*

The Old Dog's Philosophy

An old dog saw a pup chasing its tail and asked, "Why are you chasing your tail?" Said the puppy, "I have mastered philosophy; I have solved the problems of the universe which no dog before me had rightly solved; I have learned that the best thing for a dog is happiness, and that happiness is my tail. Therefore I am chasing it; and when I catch it, I shall have it!"

Said the old dog: "My son, I, too, have paid attention to the problems of the universe in my weak way, and have formed some opinions. I, too, have judged that happiness is a fine thing for a dog, and that happiness is in my tail. But I have noticed that when I chase it, it keeps running away from me; but when I go about my business, it comes after me." *Sunshine Magazine*

The Best Tranquilizer

The best tranquilizer is a clear conscience.

A Little Lump of Ego

To me there is in happiness an element of self-forgetfulness. You lose yourself in something outside yourself when you are happy; just as when you are desperately miserable you are intensely conscious of yourself, a solid little lump of ego weighing a ton. *J. B. Priestley*

Happiness

Money doesn't buy happiness, but it pays for the illusion.

Prognosis

Doctors say we can live over 100 years, but the trouble is you have to grow old to do it.

Philosophy

The best philosophy in this life is to get used to what you have and learn to like it.

Worry

Worry is like a treadmill. It can wear you to a frazzle.

The most disappointed people in the world are those who get what is coming to them.

Life's problems depend on your point of view. A bunion looks good to a chiropodist.

What the world needs is the peace that passes all misunderstanding.

Definitions

Life is a problem of whether your sin finds you out or the installment collector finds you in.

Life is described by a scientist as the metabolic activity of protoplasm. That explains everything.

Life must be worth living—the cost has douled and still most of us hang on.

Money and Misery

Money may not bring happiness, but most people like to have enough of it around so they can choose their own misery.

If and when the meek inherit the earth, it looks like they will inherit enough debt to keep them that way.

You don't have trouble with castles in the air until you try to move in.

A New Appreciation

When the cancer that later took his life was first diagnosed, Senator Richard L. Neuberger remarked upon his "new appreciation of things I once took for granted—eating lunch with a friend, scratching my cat Muffet's ears and listening for his purrs, the company of my wife, reading a book or magazine in the quiet of my bed lamp at night, raiding the refrigerator for a glass of orange juice or a slice of toast. For the first time, I think I actually am savoring life."

How to Live

If you choose to work, you will succeed; if you don't you will fail.

If you neglect your work, you will dislike it; if you do it well, you will enjoy it.

If you join little cliques, you will be self-satisfied; if you make friends widely, you will be interesting.

If you gossip, you will be slandered; if you mind your own business, you will be liked.

If you act like a boor, you will be despised; if you act like a human being, you will be respected.

If you spurn wisdom, wise people will spurn you; if you seek wisdom, they will seek you.

If you adopt a pose of boredom, you will be a bore; if you show vitality, you will be alive.

If you spend your free time playing bridge, you will be a good bridge-player; if you spend it in reading, discussing and thinking of things that matter, you will be an educated person. *Sydney Smith, President, University of Toronto, address to students*

Precious

It's good to have money, and the things that money can buy, but it's good, too, to check up once in a while and be sure you haven't lost the things money can't buy. *George Horace Lorimer*

Insincerity

The most exhausting thing in life, I have discovered, is being insincere. That is why so much social life is exhausting; one is wearing a mask. *Anne Morrow Lindbergh*

Too Little Too Late

I'm always pressed for time. An hour late and a dollar short. *Lyndon B. Johnson*

What Is Yours

Remember that what you possess in the world will be found at the day of your death to belong to another, but what you are will be yours forever. *Henry van Dyke*

Living and Giving

We make a living by what we get, but we make a life by what we give.

No Brief Candle

Life is no brief candle to me. It is a sort of splendid torch which I am permitted to hold for the moment, and I want to make it burn as brightly as possible before handing it on to future generations. *George Bernard Shaw*

14

Going Forward

That's Different
"How long have you been driving without a tail light, buddy?" demanded the policeman.

The driver jumped out, ran to the rear of his car, and gave a low moan. His distress was so great that the cop was moved to ease up on him a bit.

"Aw, come now," he said, "you don't have to take it so hard. It isn't that serious."

"It isn't?" cried the motorist. "What happened to my trailer?"

Now Drive Carefully
TRAFFIC COP (*producing notebook*): Name, please.

MOTORIST: Aloysius Alastair Cyprian.

TRAFFIC COP (*putting book away*): Well, don't let me catch you again.

Looking Ahead
"What am I to do with this?" grumbled the motorist as the police clerk handed him a receipt for his traffic fine payment.

"Keep it," the clerk advised. "When you get four of them, you get a bicycle."

Another Reason to Drive Slowly
This sign was seen on the outskirts of a small Japanese town: "Please drive carefully. Our children may be disobeying us."

We wonder why the speed cop is always so mad after he has won the race and caught you.

It Isn't Easy
The owner of a racehorse asked his jockey why he didn't ride his mount through a hole when it opened up on the final turn. "Sir," said the jockey, "did you ever try to go through a hole that was going faster than your horse?"

How Could He?

A golfer hit a new ball into the lake, another new ball out of bounds onto a highway, and another new ball into the woods.

"Why don't you use an old ball?" said the caddy.

Replied the golfer sadly, "I've never had an old ball."

Makes a Difference

Sam Goldwyn, the film magnate, accepted an invitation to join a foursome in the east for golf. The caddy handed him a driver, Sam took five lusty swings, but missed the ball each time. Grabbing the weapon again, he turned around to his partner and shrugged: "Out in California where I play, the ground is all of an inch and a half higher."

A Lesson in Statistics

In 1940, every car on the highway in California contained an average of three persons. In 1950, the average was down to two. In 1960, the average was one person. Based on a projection of these statistics, by 1990, every third car on the highway will have nobody in it.

Carelessness

It's terrible the way those careless drivers keep so close ahead of you.

New Measurements

After several years of living in a house trailer, a woman became fed up with the lack of space.

"Look at that," she said enviously, as she and her husband drove past a sprawling ranch-type house.

"Wouldn't you love to have a house that big?" she continued. "Why, I'll bet it's at least four lanes wide!"

Worry

Small signs in some taxicabs advise riders: "Don't Just Sit There, WORRY."

Worried

When the battered motorist slowly came to, his first words were, "Where am I?"

"Take it easy," the nurse whispered. "You are in 114."

The motorist waited a moment, then asked meekly, "Room or cell?"

We All Agree

When I used to walk to get some place, car drivers were a menace to the human race! But now that I, too, drive a car, I discover what fools pedestrians are.

Buying the New Car

FATHER: How many miles to a gallon?
MOTHER: What color is the upholstery?
SON: How fast will she go?
DAUGHTER: Has it a good mirror?
NEIGHBORS: How can they afford it?

Knell of Parting Day

The curfew tolls the knell of parting day. A line of cars winds slowly o'er the lea. A pedestrian plods his absentminded way, and leaves the world quite unexpectedly.

That's Different

SMITH: Don't you enjoy listening to the honk of a wild goose?
JONES: Not when he's driving an automobile.

Sunday Drivers

A Sunday driver is one who speeds up so he can get by you and slow down.

Progress

In the old days two cars could hardly pass without colliding on the narrow roads, but now we have happily advanced to great wide highways where six or eight cars can collide at once.

Speed Limit

Sign outside a Minnesota crossroad town: "Speed limit 70 M.P.H. You can't get through here too fast for us."

The speed limit is generally 55 miles in the country and 20 miles in the city, but the average driver adds them together.

We wonder how many speed records on the streets are made by people not going anywhere.

Roughing It

The modern idea of "roughing it" is driving without power steering or having a black-and-white TV set.

Signals

Judging from the number of persons who can't read traffic signals you have to assume illiteracy is increasing.

Look Out

"If you want to live long, walk," says a doctor. That depends on the traffic.

Motorists have to watch out not only for children walking but also for children driving.

Most modern parents spare the rod and Junior rides around in it.

Parking

Some time a genius will build a car like an accordion so it can be parked.

Messing Up

You can really mess up the traffic if you signal left and turn left.

New Cars

You can't drive a new car down the street without meeting everybody you owe.

Nothing seems more catastrophic than the first scratch you put on your new car.

Old Cars

One of the first things a man learns who buys a second hand car is that he wouldn't buy another one.

We always hate to trade in an old car and put so many garage repairmen out of work.

Definitions

A traffic light is a little green light that changes to red when your car approaches it.

Summer: When the highway authorities close all the regular roads and open up the detours.

Briefest moment: The time between reading the sign on the expressway and realizing you missed the exit ramp.

Car trouble: When the engine doesn't start and the payments won't stop.

Weekend: When all the cars in the country are laid out end to end.

Road hog: A person who meets you more than halfway.

Middle of the Road

A middle-of-the road policy may succeed in politics, but it gets you into lots of trouble on a highway.

We suppose in the old days there were folks that tried to cross the road ahead of the dinosaur.

If you drive too fast, you wreck the front of your car; and if you drive too slowly some one else wrecks the back.

Almost Perfect

You may not be able to fool all the people all the time, but these super-highway interchange signs come pretty close.

On Detours

All of our superhighways fall into one of two classes: overcrowded or under construction.

Reckless

A reckless driver is a person who passes you on the highway in spite of all you can do.

A reckless driver is seldom wreckless for very long.

A Consumer with a Car

The easiest thing for a consumer with a car to run into is debt.

There is an automobile for every 2½ persons. The missing half is the pedestrian who has been run over.

There's a line on the ocean where, by crossing it, you can lose a day. But, there's one on the highway where you can do even better than that.

Automobiles may have welded bodies, but there still are plenty of nuts in them.

A bad combination—100 horse power under the hood and no horse sense behind the wheel.

All the world may love a lover, but he is a poor risk driving on a fast highway.

If all the cars at a busy crossroads were laid end to end, some dumbbell would pull out and try to pass.

Progress

A cloverleaf intersection is an ingenious road-building device which enables a driver to get on four wrong roads in the time it used to take him to get on one.

Many freeways have three lanes: a left lane, a right lane, and the one you're trapped in when you see your exit.

An Idea

Perhaps we ought to find a way to make cars operate on honey instead of gasoline. A gallon of nectar, says the National Geographic Society, can fuel a bee four million miles at a speed of seven miles an hour. And no air pollution.

And on the Left

Leader of a flock of geese to the bird following: "Stop that infernal honking—if you want to pass, pass!"

Up in the Air

Now that we travel miles up in the air we know that there are no silver linings on the other side of the clouds either.

Not Too Hard

The owner of a midget car drove to a filling station and asked for a pint of gas and two ounces of oil.

"Right," said the attendant. "And would you like me to sneeze in the tires?"

Can't Fuel All the People

Sign seen at a service station during the gasoline shortage: "We can fuel some of the people some of the time, but we can't fuel all the people all the time."

Danger!

The first baby carriage was made by Charles Burton in 1884 and used in New York City. People in those days protested violently that the carriage was dangerous to pedestrians!

Exercise

Walking isn't a lost art. How else can we get to the garage?

15

Wish I'd Said That

Getting Attention
To draw attention to yourself, it's hard to beat a big mistake.

What Goes Down
Only an amateur gardener believes that what goes down must come up.

Mary Todd
Asked one day whether his wife, Mary Todd, came from a good family, Abraham Lincoln replied: "The very best. Why, the Todds spell their name with two d's; one was good enough for God!"

Human Beings
No two human beings are alike and both of them are glad of it.

There is no such thing as an average man. Just ask one to admit it.

One of the worst things about life is not how nasty the nasty people are. You know that already. It is how nasty the nice people can be. *Anthony Powell*

Definitions
A pessimist is a person who thinks the world is against him—and it is.

An optimist is a person who wants you to cheer up when things are going his way.

Machines
Machines are so nearly human that they do things without using any intelligence.

Fools
You can fool all the people some of the time, but you can fool yourself all the time.

Some people have so little good judgment they take a chance every time they use it.

There is a bigger fool than the fellow who knows it all: it's the fellow who will argue with him.

Best Way to Win
The best way to win an argument is to avoid it.

Advice
Often when we ask for advice, what we really want is approval.

No wise man needs advice and no ignoramus wants it.

Why is it that most people give others better advice than they give themselves?

Tower of Babel
It's just possible the Tower of Babel was the first United Nations.

True in Life Generally
There are two kinds of nations in the world—the good and the bad. The classifying is done by the good.

Something to It
Some nations are getting ahead in the world because they are willing to work for less to get more.

Strange
Throughout history the greatest menace to civilization has been the civilized nations.

International Conscience
International conscience is the still small voice that tells a country when another country is the stronger.

No Answers
The world's political leaders know all the questions, but none of the answers.

Diplomacy
Diplomacy is the ability to take something and act as if you were giving it away.

Not Particular

One of the stories I like to tell about Ev Dirksen, one that he sort of told himself, was linked with his desire for harmony and unity in his Party.

He said whenever there was a lack of this it reminded him of two deacons, one a Republican and one a Democrat. They were meeting together in a little Illinois church praying, and the Democratic deacon started first, and he said, "O Lord, make us Democrats unlike the Republicans; make us hang together in accord; make us hang together in concord."

Whereupon the Republican deacon said, "O Lord, any old cord will do."
Walter J. Hickel

Good Advice

It's pretty difficult to put your foot in your mouth if you keep it closed.

You learn more by listening than by talking, but it isn't nearly as much fun.

A man's temper improves the more he doesn't use it.

Flattery is a perfume to be smelled, but not swallowed.

The flattery that gets you nowhere is what you listen to.

You may be a fine, upstanding citizen, but it makes no difference to a banana.

The Sucker Wants to Get Rich

It's funny how a sucker can find a swindler when a skilled detective can not.

Different Here

In heaven the sheep and goats are divided, but down here the sheep are the goats.

Folly

There are more fools than sages, and even in a sage there is more folly than wisdom. *Nicolas Chamfort*

The more stupid we are, the less patience we have with others.

When a man hasn't enough money to act silly, don't give him credit for having sense.

Swedish Proverb

A peacock has too little in its heads, too much in its tail.

Problems

Two problems face the people of every big city—where to park and where to jump.

If you can't state the problem in a few simple sentences, you probably don't know what the problem is.

Blame Not

Diving and finding no pearl in the sea, blame not the ocean, the fault is in thee. *Chinese Proverb*

Keeping Busy

A good number of people keep busy in life perfecting their faults.

Faults & Weaknesses

Only the rich can call their faults and weaknesses eccentricities.

There is so much good in the worst of us, and so much bad in the best of, that it's hard to tell which one of us ought to try to reform the rest of us.

He who has nothing but virtues is not much better than he who has nothing but faults. *Swedish Proverb*

Being young is a fault which improves daily.

Think of your own faults the first part of the night when you are awake, and the faults of others the latter part of the night when you are asleep. *Chinese Proverb*

If you feel that you have no faults—that makes another one.

He Who Knows Most

The wise know too well their weakness to assume infallibility; and he who knows most, knows best how little he knows. *Thomas Jefferson*

Fault Finding

Nothing is easier than fault finding; no talent, no self-denial, no brains, no character are required to set up in the grumbling business. *Robert West*

The Literary Beat

We kind of like these three immortal quotes that strayed our way:
"To be is to do."—Camus
"To do is to be."—Sartre
"Do be do be do."—Bing Crosby

Doing Nothing

Bing Crosby: "There's nothing in the world I wouldn't do for that guy, and there's nothing in the world he wouldn't do for me. We spend our lives doing nothing for each other."

Still Guilty

A popular songwriter says it is a mystery to him how he does it. Ignorance of the law is no excuse.

Trouble

If nobody knows the trouble you've seen, you don't live in a small town.

A Problem

Remember when a magazine sent Robert Benchley on an assignment to Venice and he wired back, "Streets full of water. Please advise"?

Rumors

People will believe anything if you whisper it.

A rumor is a breeze stirred up by a couple of windbags.

Taking Criticism

I love criticism just so long as it's unqualified praise. *Noel Coward*

Only people who do things get criticized.

Don't worry about what people think of you. They aren't thinking of you, but of themselves.

If you worry about what people think of you, it shows you think more of their opinion than your own.

Pennsylvania Dutch

Don't eat yourself full, there's cake back yet.
The pie is all but the cake is yet.
The beans is all already, so many got et.
Jane, eat your mouth empty before you say.
Don't horn the machine so, you'll blow the baby awake.
Get out and tie the dog loose.
Papa went to town mit himself alone.

Golf

Golf for most of us is just another method of beating around the bush.

Correct

A teacher was taking her first golf lesson. "Is the word spelled 'put' or 'putt'?" she asked the instructor.

" 'Putt' is correct," he replied. " 'Put' means to place a thing where you want it. 'Putt' means a vain attempt to do the same thing."

Leisure

Nothing gives a person more leisure than always being on time for appointments.

Gratitude

Gratitude is the memory of the heart. *Jean Baptiste Massieu*

Growing Old

Hardening of the heart makes one grow old faster than hardening of the arteries.

First Things First

The older I get, the more wisdom I find in the ancient rule of taking first things first—a process which often reduces the most complex human problems to manageable proportions. *Dwight D. Eisenhower*

Loans

Sign in a finance company window: "Loans—for those who have everything but haven't paid for all of it yet."

Fewer people would be in debt if they didn't spend what their friends think they make.

If you want to avoid undue excitement, live within your income.

Few people care to be such misers as to live within their own incomes.

A father is a banker provided by nature.

Some People

Some people expect it to rain when they thunder.

Some people are not the life of the party until they leave.

Some folks seem to think they can eat their cake and then have yours, too.

Solitude

The person who is certain that everything should be done his way should first be even more certain that he loves solitude.

I love to be alone. I never found the companion that was so companionable as solitude. *Henry David Thoreau*

Anne Morrow Lindbergh made this observation: "If one sets aside time for a business appointment, a trip to the hairdresser, a social engagement, or a shopping expedition, that time is accepted as inviolable. But if one says, 'I cannot come because that is my hour to be alone,' one is considered rude, egotistical, or strange. What a commentary on our civilization, when being alone is considered suspect; when one has to apologize for it, make excuses, hide the fact that one practices it—like a secret vice."

Swedish Proverb

No one has so big a house that he does not need a good neighbor.

Housekeeping Hint

The way to keep your closets clean is to get a bigger garage.

Modern Art

In modern art, things are never as bad as they are painted.

It is said that painters of modern art paint for their own pleasure. Many of them seem easy to please.

Bargains

A bargain is something you can't use at a price you cannot resist.

He who buys what he doesn't need steals from himself. *Swedish Proverb*

Be Careful What You Say

A scientist says woman's foot is getting larger, but maybe it just seems that way because she puts it down harder.

Cheer Up

Whenever you feel neglected, remember Whistler's father.

Maybe Later

Uncle Joe thinks this is a poor time for the meek to inherit the earth.

Typical of Life

One dog barks at something; the rest bark at him. *Chinese Proverb*

Dog

A dog teaches a boy fidelity, perserverance and to turn around three times before lying down. *Robert Benchley*

Bird

I am free to admit that I am the kind of man who would never notice an oriole building a nest, unless it came and built it in my hat in the hat room of the club. *Stephen Leacock*

Impediment

Two men were discussing a mutual acquaintance.

"Nice fellow," said one, "but have you noticed how he always lets his friends pick up the check?"

"Yes," replied the other. "He has a terrible impediment in his reach."

Manners

Good manners enable you to wait in silence while the loud-mouth gets served.

Food

Part of the secret of success in life is to eat what you like and let the food fight it out inside. *Mark Twain*

Sage Advice

Don't throw away the old bucket until you know whether the new one holds water. *Swedish Proverb*

A person who thinks too much of himself isn't thinking enough.

Athletes

You have heard of the rambling wreck from Georgia Tech. Well, I was known as the total loss from Holy Cross. *Robert Delvaney, Athletic Director of the University of Nebraska*

Never So Confused

A man never becomes so confused in his thinking that he can't see the other fellow's duty.

A Mirror

The world is like a mirror, reflecting what you do; and if your face is smiling, it smiles right back at you.

Useless

No one ever gets very far pacing the floor.

A customer who asks the waiter for a piece of meat without fat, gristle or bone should order eggs.

Agriculture

Blessed be agriculture! If one does not have too much of it. *Charles Dudley Warner*

A chrysanthemum by any other name would look the same—and be easier to spell.

Him Who Waits

All things come to him who waits—but not soon enough to do much good.

Agreeable

Nobody can be as agreeable as an uninvited guest. *Frank McKinney Hubbard*

Guests should not forget to go home. *Swedish Proverb*

Wealth

Well, yes, you could say we have independent means. *John D. Rockefeller, III*

Second Hand Diamonds

As Mark Twain said, "It's better to have old second hand diamonds than none at all."

16

For Better or Worse

What We Thought

Someone says that dark-haired people marry first. We always thought it was the light-headed ones.

Is That Nice?

"Tell me, Mr. Smith," said the marriage counselor, after several sessions, "did you wake up grouchy this morning?"

"No," said Mr. Smith. "I let her sleep."

Naturally

A judge asked a defendant why he struck his wife. The man replied, "Her back was turned, the broom was handy, and the back door was open."

Sounds Reasonable

"Your finances are in terrible shape," the banker stated. "Your checking account is overdrawn, your loan is overdue. Why do you allow your wife to spend more money than you make?"

"Frankly," replied the man with a deep sigh, "because I'd rather argue with you than with her."

Where the Money Went

Jack Spratt could eat no fat;
His wife could eat no lean.
So, you know,
They spent their dough,
For TVs and gasoline.

Man or Mouse

President Eisenhower told this one: Three men asked a fourth to join them for a golf game. He declined, saying he had to go home to his wife.

"Are you a man," asked one of the group, "or a mouse?"

"I'm a man," said the reluctant one, "Mary's afraid of mice!"

He Was Lucky

The bride had news for her husband when he returned from work.

"I feel terrible," she sobbed. "I was pressing your suit and burned a hole in the trousers."

"Don't worry," said the husband, "I have another pair of pants for that suit."

"Yes, I know," said the wife, " and it's lucky you have. I used them to patch the hole."

Of Course Not

A man was telling his friend about his family. "When I go home at night," he said, "everything is ready for me, my slippers, my pipe, the easy chair in the corner with the light on, my book open at the same place I left it the night before—and always plenty of hot water."

"I understand all that stuff about the slippers and easy chair and book and the pipe," his friend said, "but why the hot water?"

"Well," the man said, "my family loves me. You don't think they are going to make me wash dishes in cold water, do you?"

Marriage

When I was young, there was a song that went: "We will live on love and kisses, letting Cupid wash the dishes"—students, I have been married 35 years and never once has Cupid done our dishes. *Dr. Louis Evans, addressing students at Pennsylvania State University*

Not Married Yet

When one of Martha's little friends came to see her, she found Martha playing with her new housekeeping set.

"Are you washing dishes?" asked the friend.

"Yes," replied Martha, "and I'm drying them, too, 'cause I'm not married yet."

Best Way

The best way for a housewife to have a few minutes to herself at the close of the day is to start doing the dishes.

Has This Happened to You?

"I just found a letter in a woman's handwriting in the pocket of your brown suit," the young wife told her husband.

"In my pocket?" answered the flustered husband. "Why, I certainly don't know how it got there!"

"Well I do," said the wife in sweet tones, "I wrote it and gave it to you to mail three days ago."

Just Call

Mother, tucking child into bed: "Now, darling, if you need anything during the night, just call Mother, and Daddy will come."

Easy Question

ADAM: Eve, do you really love me?

EVE: Who else?

Bororos Say "I Do"

One of the most interesting Indian tongues in Brazil, for Americans, is that of the Bororos, partly because it is the only language in the world other than English in which "I" is "I."

Also "she" means "woman" or "mother"; "baba-do" means "to babble."

Oddly, "weary" means "wife" and "weary-do" means to get married.

Sin ━

A young minister was preaching a sermon on sin. This was his popular topic. He preached on it every Sunday. He said, "For all have sinned and come short of the glory of God." Well, that's true, the Bible says that, but the people were falling asleep. And he figured, "I'll ask a rhetorical question, I'll wake them up this way." He said, "Is there anyone here this morning who has never sinned? Stand up!" About three-quarters of the way back a person was standing. He said, "Obviously, sir, you didn't hear my question correctly. I asked, 'Is there any person here who has *never* sinned?'" The man calmly said, "No, but I'm standing on behalf of my wife's first husband." *John A. Huffman, Jr.*

Checks

"Who is your favorite author?"

"My husband."

"What does he write?"

"Checks."

Didn't Know Why Not

WIFE: You know, dear, you don't seem as well dressed as you were when we were married, ten years ago.

HUSBAND: I don't know why not. I'm wearing the same suit.

Rummage Sale

"Dear," the little woman reported, "a man came today gathering contributions for the old clothes drive."

"Did you give him anything?" asked the husband.

"Yes, honey," she replied. "I gave him that ten-year-old suit of yours and that dress I bought last month."

The Average Man

He is 39 around the chest, 40 around the waist, 96 around the golf course, 132 around the bowling alleys, seldom around when needed, and a nuisance around the house.

The average man is proof enough that a woman can really take a joke.

Not Easy

A real estate agent was showing an old farmhouse to a woman prospect who made a few sketches on a pad and admitted, "I could do a lot with that house." But then she added wistfully, "On the other hand, I believe I said the same thing the first time I saw my husband."

Amazing

Wife to husband as the tailor measured his waist: "It's quite amazing when you realize that a Douglas fir with that much girth would be ninety feet tall!"

Diplomacy

A woman should try to make her husband feel he is boss of the home, even if he's really just chairman of the fund-raising committee.

No Substitutes

"Sorry, we don't have potted geraniums," the clerk said, and then added helpfully, "Could you use African violets?"

"No," replied the husband sadly. "It was geraniums my wife told me to water while she was gone."

It Isn't Easy

Said the sweet young thing, tripping up to the bank cashier's window: "Tell me how to make out a check so that the money will come out of my husband's half of our joint bank account."

Gift Wrap

Father watching his daughter select the most expensive wedding gown: "I don't mind giving you away, but must I gift wrap you?"

The Other Side

"Judge, your honor," complained the angry woman to the court, "this no-account husband of mine drinks."

"Yes, sir, judge, I do drink some," admitted the man. "But, judge, that woman don't treat me right. Why, I pawned the kitchen stove to get a little money and she didn't miss it for two weeks."

Definitions
Old-fashioned wife: One who tried to make one husband last a lifetime.

Marriage: An institution which teaches man frugality, regularity, temperance and other virtues he wouldn't need if he stayed single.

More about Marriage
Courtship is what makes a man spoon, but marriage is what makes him fork over.

The honeymoon is over when bushels of kisses are reduced to little pecks.

Marriage not only brings a lot of change into a person's life, but it takes a lot out, too.

Marriage is a mutual partnership, in which either the husband or the wife can be the mute.

If marriage makes two persons one, it must not take two to make a quarrel.

After twenty awed years of married life, all troubles look smaller.

When they asked the movie actress how long she had been married, she said, "This time or all together?"

That Will Hold Him
After the honeymoon, the new husband asked his bride, "You don't mind if I point out a few of your little defects, do you?"
"Not at all, dear," replied the bride. "It's those little defects that kept me from getting a better husband."

Women's Lib
Mrs. Jones, full of enthusiasm, had gone in for politics. One night she returned late and sank into a comfortable chair.
"Everything's grand," she said. "We'll sweep the country!"
Mr. Jones looked around wearily and said, "Why not start with the dining room?"

She Knew
"If I had a million dollars, do you know where I'd be?" asked Bert.
"I sure do—you'd be on our honeymoon," answered Gert.

141

He Asked for It

"Surely," insisted the marriage counselor, "you must have said something to start the terrible argument."

"Not really," the husband replied. "My wife had tried a new recipe for dinner. When she asked how I liked it, all I said, was, 'It's okay, but it will never take the place of food.'"

Motherly Advice

"What do you give a man who has everything?" queried daughter.

"Encouragement—lots of it," advised her mother.

Compliment

"Does your wife ever pay you any compliments?" asked the curious bachelor.

"Only in the winter," was the nonchalant answer.

"In the winter? How do you mean?"

"When the fire gets low, she says, 'Alexander, the grate!'"

Things Change

An old man neglected to assist his wife into the bus. "John," she said reprovingly, "you are not so gallant as when you were a boy." To which he replied, "No, and you are not so buoyant as when you were a gal."

It isn't long before a June husband forgets how to drive with one hand.

The cure for love at first sight is to take another look.

Just about the time a woman thinks her work is all done, she becomes a grandmother.

Advice

Try praising your wife—even if it does frighten her at first.

If at first you don't succeed, do it the way your wife told you.

Expensive Pullover

When the woman driver made an illegal turn, the officer ordered her to pull over and gave her a ticket. Anxious to keep her husband from learning the true facts during his monthly audit of her checkbook, she marked the stub, "One pullover, $25."

Still No Agreement

HUSBAND: In our six years of marriage we haven't been able to agree on anything.

WIFE: It's been seven years, dear.

142

Best Way

The best way to remember your wife's birthday is to forget it once.

The young man said he knew his girl could keep a secret, because they had been engaged for weeks before even he new anything about it.

True Love

The course of true love isn't smooth, but don't get the idea that the detours are smoother.

Some people make the mistake of marrying for better or worse but not for good.

Many couples are unhappily married, but fortunately don't know it.

A Problem

Harried wife to husband and children: "Well, I worked out a budget. But one of us will have to go."

Two persons can now live as cheaply as a family of ten used to.

He Really Loved Her

FATHER: When he proposed, didn't you ask him to see me?

DAUGHTER: Yes, and he said he had seen you several times, but he loved me just the same.

No Quarrel

You say you never had a quarrel with your wife?

Never. She goes her way and I go hers.

The Bridegroom

Unaccustomed as he was to public speaking, the bridegroom was flustered when they called on him for a speech. He steadied himself by placing his hand on the bride's shoulder as he stammered: "This has been unexpectedly forced upon me."

Good Course

Betty, the five-year-old, met the caller at the door. "Alice isn't here," she replied to the caller's inquiry about her big sister. "She's gone to her class."

"What class does she go to, little sister?" asked the caller.

"Well, Alice is going to get married, you know, and she's taking lessons in domestic silence."

Smart Woman

Any man who thinks he is smarter than his wife is married to a very smart woman.

Bachelors

All reformers are bachelors. *George Moore*

The biggest mystery to a married man is what a bachelor does with his money.

A bachelor has no one to share his troubles. Why should he? He hasn't any.

Typical Experience?

The husband put in a flagstone walk from the house to the street, and when he was all finished he called his wife to come for a look.

"It's terrible," she said. "The colors don't match; it's too narrow and the stones are crooked."

Weary and disappointed, the husband asked, "How is it for length?"

Slight Bias

I may be a little like this friend of mine down in Indiana some years back. He married Tilly. He had a long and happy life with her until she died. He buried her out in the local cemetery. A year later he married Milly, and she lived six or eight years, and when she died, he buried her six feet away from Tilly.

And when he died, they opened his strong box in the bank and looked into the will, and it said, "Bury me between Milly and Tilly, but tilt me a little toward Tilly."

17

Genius at Work

Scribbled All Over It

A man who was very much interested in old books ran into an unbookish acquaintance of his who had just thrown away an old Bible which had been packed away in the attic of his ancestral home for generations. The latter happened to mention it. "Somebody named Guten-something had printed it," he said.

"Not Gutenberg!" gasped the book lover. "You idiot! You've thrown away one of the first books ever printed. A copy sold at auction recently for over $400,000!"

The other man was unmoved. "My copy wouldn't have brought a dime," he announced. "Some fellow named Martin Luther had scribbled all over it."

Smart

A man saw his pal poring over a chessboard. Opposite him sat a dog.

"Hey, what's going on?" he asked.

"Just playing chess with my dog," replied the pal.

"You're kidding! Whoever heard of a dog playing chess!"

"You're not only hearing—you're watching one play." He made a move, which the dog pondered, then countered.

"Well, I'll be!" exclaimed the droppin'-in. "That's the smartest dog I've ever seen!"

"Oh, I don't know about that," replied the player; "I've beaten him four out of five games."

To the Head of the Class

The third grade was being given a course in first aid. The question was asked: "What would you do if you had a younger brother or sister who swallowed a house key?"

After a pause of thoughtful silence, one of the youngsters answered, "I'd climb in through the window!"

Smart Fellow

Then there was the fellow who discovered a way to hammer nails without hitting his thumb. He had his wife hold the nail.

Not Yet Perfect
Gutzon Borglum, the sculptor who created the tremendous Mount Rushmore Memorial, was once asked if he considered his work perfect in detail.

"Not today," he replied. "The nose of Washington is an inch too long. It's better that way, though. It will erode to be exactly right in 10,000 years."

Show Me
Show me a man whose feet are firmly planted on solid ground, and I'll show you a man about to try a difficult putt.

The Trouble
The trouble with most of us is that we discuss too many subjects authoritatively.

Good Is Not the Word
Franz Liszt, no less a diplomat than a musician, had a stock reply for young ladies, particularly pretty ones, who demanded unmerited praise of their talents.

"Maestro," the young things would inquire, "do you not think I have a good voice?"

"Ah, my dear young lady," Liszt would reply, his voice ringing with enthusiasm, "good is not the word!"

Definition
Genius: A fellow who is a crackpot, until he hits the jackpot.

Wrong Identity
I always thought I was Jeanne d'Arc and Bonaparte. How little one knows oneself. *Charles de Gaulle, replying to a speaker who compared him to Robespierre.*

True Greatness
No man has achieved true greatness who can count his enemies on his fingers.

A Token of Friendship
An American businessman had always wanted to own a real Picasso. He obtained permission to visit the artist's studio. Hoping to flatter the painter into a generous mood, the visitor praised everything. Finally he saw a simple line drawing protruding from a wastebasket. He retrieved it reverently. "How much is this?" he asked.

"As a token of friendship," Picasso replied, "take it for $35,000." *Boston Globe*

A Diplomat

The wit and charm of the late Adlai Stevenson made him a constant target for autograph-seekers. Once, as he left the United Nations Building in New York and was as usual surrounded by young admirers, a small, elderly lady in the crowd finally succeeded in approaching him.

"Please, Mr. Ambassador," she said, holding out a piece of paper, "your autograph for a very, very old lady."

"Delighted!" Stevenson smiled, "Where is she?"

Qualified

Voltaire, the French satirist, was informed that a bitter enemy had died in London.

"You know," said his informant, speaking of the deceased, "when all is said and done, he was a good man."

"He was a great man," corrected Voltaire. Then he added, "That is, if he is really dead."

Inspiration

Peter Altenberg tells how somebody once asked Anton Bruckner: "Master, how, when, where, did you think of the divine motif of your Ninth Symphony?"

"Well, it was like this," said Bruckner. "I walked up the Kahlenberg, and when it got hot and I got hungry, I sat down by a little brook and unpacked my Swiss cheese. And just as I opened the greasy paper, that tune popped into my head!" *Robert E. Luccock, Christian Herald*

Exercise

Don't you ever take any exercise?" a friend asked Oscar Wilde one day. "Indeed I do," he replied. "I have breakfast in bed."

Well Informed

At a function George Bernard Shaw was attending, he had been bored to death by the ceaseless conversation of a man who was trying to impress him. Eventually the man paused for a moment.

"You know," Shaw quickly observed, "between the two of us we know everything there is to know."

"How's that?" asked the man.

"Well," replied Shaw, "you seem to know everything except that you're a bore. And I know that!"

We've Met This Guide

The museum guide was just finishing the tour: "And here, ladies and gentlemen, at the close, this splendid Greek statue. Note the noble way in which the neck supports the head, the splendid curve of the shoulders, and ladies and gentlemen, note the natural way in which the opened hand is outstretched, as if to emphasize: 'Don't forget a tip for the guide.' "

We've Thought the Same

"By George, old chap, when I look at one of your paintings I stand and wonder . . ." mused the art critic.

"How I do it?" queried the artist eagerly.

"No; why."

Absentminded Genius

Albert Einstein, writes Joseph Cassidy, once invited some friends to go to the Metropolitan Opera with him. Halfway through the second act, he became bored and excused himself to get some fresh air.

Once outside, he got into his car and drove home, forgetting his friends whom he had driven in. They had to take a late train home.

Modest

Sir Arthur Eddington, a British astronomer, was once asked: "Is it true, Sir Arthur, that you are one of the three men in the world who understand Einstein's theory of relativity?"

The astronomer appeared reluctant to answer.

"Forgive me," said his questioner, "I should have realized a man of your modesty would find such a question embarrassing."

"Not at all," said Eddington. "I was just trying to think who the third could be."

Problems

It would be very nice if we could save up our problems for a brainy day.

Not a Trifle

Michelangelo was working on a statue one afternoon when some friends visited him. A month later they returned and found him still working on the same statue.

"What have you done since our last visit?" one asked.

"Oh, I've smoothed a line here, and polished an arm, taken a few flakes of marble from the forehead, and so on," replied the great artist.

"But those are only trifles! Is that all you've done?"

"True, they are but trifles," Michelangelo gravely responded, "but trifles make perfection, and perfection is no trifle."

The Whole Is Important

Dickens put the new moon in the East in one of his books. In another he had schoolmaster Squeers' unfortunate boys hoeing turnips in the dead of winter. In penning the immortal story of Robinson Crusoe, the author, Daniel Defoe, had his hero fill his pockets with biscuits while in a state of nudity. In *King Solomon's Mines* Rider Haggard described an eclipse of the new moon.

These masters of story telling, in spite of their universally acknowledged skill in their peculiar art, were either absentminded at times, or were a bit careless about details.

Millions of delighted readers have perused all of the tales mentioned above, but how many ever noticed the errors? One could perhaps draw several morals from the foregoing facts. One which might be overlooked is, the whole of things is more important than any part. *Sunshine Magazine*

Loneliness

Shakespeare, Leonardo da Vinci, Benjamin Franklin, and Lincoln never saw a movie, heard a radio, or looked at TV. They had "loneliness" and knew what to do with it. They were not afraid of being lonely because they knew that was when the creative mood in them would work. *Carl Sandburg*

Art

Art is a collaboration between God and the artist, and the less the artist does the better. *André Gide*

Lincoln's Source

One of the things that has surprised scholars about Abraham Lincoln is that a man of the people, without the education of the schools, should have been able to write English that is marvelous in its clarity and simplicity, in its dignity and majesty. The Gettysburg Address and the Second Inaugural straight away passed into the list of classics in our language. One explanation is the source from which Lincoln learned his speech. As a boy and man he possessed and read the Bible until the spirit of its simple dignity passed into his own words, and its phrases were fixed in his memory for effective use when he was an adult.

Fundamental Qualities

The great French Marshal, Ferdinand Foch, once said, "The fundamental qualities for good execution of a plan are, first, naturally, intelligence; then discernment and judgment, which enable one to recognize the best methods to attain it; then singleness of purpose; and lastly, what is most essential of all, will—stubborn will."

Dedication

He who would do some great thing in this short life must apply himself to work with such a concentration of his forces as to idle spectators, who live only to amuse themselves, looks like insanity. *Parkman*

Advice

A young composer once came to Mozart for advice on how to develop creatively.

"Begin writing simple things first," Mozart told him. "Songs, for example."

"But you composed symphonies when you were only a child," the man exclaimed.

"Ah," Mozart answered, "but I didn't go to anybody to find out how to become a composer!"

A Champion

Jack Dempsey, former world's heavyweight boxing champion: "A champion is one who gets up when he can't."

Be Displeased

Be always displeased with what thou art, if thou desirest to attain to what thou art not; for where thou hast pleased thyself, there thou abidest. Always add, always walk, always proceed. Neither stand still, nor go back, nor deviate. *Augustine*

Dream

You see things and you say "Why?" But I dream things that never were, and I say "Why not?" *George Bernard Shaw*

His Handicap Helped Him

Many famous people have turned handicaps into blessings. It is said that Arturo Toscanini owed his success, or at least his chance at success, to the fact that he was very nearsighted. At nineteen, he was playing cello in an orchestra, and as he couldn't see the music on the stand, he had to memorize it.

One day the orchestra leader became ill, and young Toscanini was the only member of the orchestra who knew the score. So he conducted it without a score and the audience gave him a good hand for it—and audiences kept on doing it. If he hadn't been nearsighted, he might have continued playing cello in small European orchestras, instead of becoming one of the greatest orchestra conductors who ever lived. *Sunshine Magazine*

Life's Troubles

Rembrandt's domestic troubles served only to heighten and deepen his art, and perhaps his best canvases were painted under stress of circumstances and in sadness of heart. His life is another proof, if needed, that the greatest truths and beauties are to be seen only through tears. Too bad for the man! But the world—the same ungrateful, selfish world that has always lighted its torch at the funeral pyres of genius—is the gainer. *John C. Van Dyke*

Sold Too Soon

When Edgar Allan Poe finally sold his famous poem, "The Raven," he was paid ten dollars for it. Now the original manuscript is valued at a quarter of a million dollars.

A Truly Great Man

I believe that the first test of a truly great man is his humility. I do not mean, by humility, doubt of his own power. But really great men have a curious feeling that the greatness is not in them, but through them. And they see something divine in every other man and are endlessly, foolishly, incredibly merciful. *John Ruskin*

Humility

Some of the greatest men I have had the privilege of knowing not only are the most humble, but are those who express their humility by becoming actual servants in their relationships with others. *Mark O. Hatfield*

He Works at It

A year ago I had a sensational experience, for I was seated in a large amphitheater in Jerusalem with about 1,200 delegates to a world convention—individuals from many, many foreign countries and a large number of people from the United States. We listened to many boring lectures and some pretty exciting lectures, but I think the most fascinating experience was the beginning of that convention. Gathered in that large amphitheater we watched a procession of individuals representing each of the great countries of the world as they came into that auditorium. We heard the former prime minister of Israel, David Ben-Gurion, then the Israeli Philharmonic Orchestra played some music in the background, and center stage stepped the great basso of the Metropolitan Opera, Jerome Hines. He sang "The Holy City." Chills ran up and down my spine as I listened to him.

That noon I was privileged to talk with the young man who conducted the orchestra. We talked about Jerome Hines, and I made this statement: "Oh, to be gifted as is Jerome Hines, oh, to have that kind of voice." And I was quickly put into my place, as this young man said, "John, Jerome Hines is gifted, yes, but he works at it." He said, "What you don't realize is that this morning, at six o'clock, Jerome Hines came here to this amphitheater, and for three hours he warmed up, doing vocal exercises, preparing his voice to sing for four to five short minutes." I was sleeping at that time of the morning. I came there at ten o'clock and heard him sing. And I'll never forget the words: "Gifted, but he works at it!" *John A. Huffman, Jr.*

Who Cares?

Michelangelo came down from the scaffolding to complain to a helper. "I am not satisfied with the eye on that one cherub."

The helper said, "Who cares? Nobody will ever see it."

"But I will see it," replied Michelangelo.

That is where you can start. You can't change the whole world, but you can monitor yourself. In disciplining yourself, you can become a capacious person who changes others. No one is an island; we are all part of the mainland. *Bryant M. Kirkland*

Forgiveness

When Leonardo da Vinci was working on his painting "The Last Supper," he became angry with a certain man. Losing his temper, he lashed the other fellow with bitter words. Returning to his canvas, he attempted to work on the face of Jesus, but was unable to do so. He was so upset, he could not compose himself for the painstaking work. Finally he put down his tools and sought out the man and asked his forgiveness. The man accepted his apology, and Leonardo was able to return to his workshop and finish painting the face of Jesus.

A Peasant Woman

The art of interpretation is great and rare: Raphael was walking along a road in the outskirts of Italy upon one occasion; he met a peasant woman passing by with a shawl on her head, lapping over one shoulder. He paused; there he saw motherhood, patience, love, sympathy, courage, suffering; he asked her to go to his studio, and he placed upon the canvas a work of art that thousands of people go thousands of miles yearly to see, the "Sistine Madonna." *Sunshine Magazine*

They Were Out of Step

John Keats lived just 26 years, yet his poetry will live forever, much of it equal to that of Shakespeare. Franz Schubert died at 31. In those 31 years, he wrote more than 110 musical compositions, more than 60 of them lyric songs of rare beauty.

Here is a boy so ugly and ridiculously clothed that he was tormented by his schoolmates. He spent his time reading to forget his misery. At 18, he worked as a bricklayer. But he finally won the acclaim and esteem of England. He was honored by Queen Elizabeth I and decorated by King James I. His name was Ben Jonson, and he was one of the most brilliant playwrights England ever produced.

Here is a boy so ugly and ridiculously clothed that he was regarded as a stupid blockhead in the village school. When he finally got a degree from college, he was the lowest on the list. He was rejected for the ministry. He tried law with the same result. He borrowed a suit of clothes to take an examination as a hospital mate, failed, and pawned his clothes. He lived in garrets, failing at everything he tried. Only one thing he wanted to do—write. This he did and rose above the handicaps of illness, poverty, and obscurity to high rank among the greatest writers of all time. He was Oliver Goldsmith.

The world is waiting for people out of step—men who dare think, men who refuse to be grasshoppers, men who dare stand on their own feet. *Sunshine Magazine*

Intelligence Test?

One test of intelligence might be to take everything out of the bathroom medicine chest and tell what it's for.

Comfort

An occasional weakness in a great man is a comfort to the rest of us.

But I Haven't Done It!

When Frederic Remington was an art student at Yale someone asked him what he intended to paint when he finished his schooling. Remington answered: "I think I shall go West and paint Indians."

His questioner scoffed at such an ambition. "Many men have already painted Indians," he said.

"Perhaps they have," Remington replied, "but I have never painted them."

The old West owes a great deal to Remington's confidence in his own ability to keep it forever alive in pictures. After Yale he went West and purchased a ranch, which he operated for several years. There he learned to know the men and the horses of the West, and he captured something of its free and dangerous spirit. When he finally began to paint Indians he knew from close observation that they were not all alike, that different tribes had characteristics peculiar to themselves. So close was his observation and so true his artistic skill that any old-time Westerner looking at pictures of Indians by Remington could say: "These are Apaches. That is a Sioux." *Sunshine Magazine*

Inspiration

The great composer does not set to work because he is inspired, but becomes inspired because he is working. Beethoven, Wagner, Bach, and Mozart settled down day after day to the job in hand with as much regularity as an accountant settles down each day in his figures. They didn't waste time waiting for inspiration. *Ernest Newman*

18

Is The Country Still Here?

Indispensable

Calvin Coolidge had humor and sense enough to escape that exaggeration of the ego which afflicts a good many men in positions of leadership. Awakening from a nap in the middle of a presidential executive day, he opened his eyes, grinned, and asked a friend: "Is the country still here?"

Our Birthright

I am a living witness that any one of your children may look to come here as my father's child has. It is in order that each one of you may have, through this free government, an open field and a fair chance for your industry, enterprise, and intelligence, that you may all have equal privileges in the race of life, with all its desirable human aspirations. It is for this the struggle should be maintained that we may not lose our birthright. The nation is worth fighting for to secure such an inestimable jewel. *Abraham Lincoln*

Retired Presidents

"What do retired U.S. Presidents do?" asked a lady some years back. "Madam, we spend our time taking pills, and dedicating libraries," explained the venerable expert on the subject, *Herbert Hoover, 31st U.S. President*

A New Worry

When you think about having a woman for President, that's no problem. What's worrisome is the thought of having a man for First Lady.

Freedom

They have a freedom I would personally dearly love. *Dwight Eisenhower, on White House squirrels*

Public Figures

You will feel that you are no longer clothing yourself; you are dressing a public monument. *Eleanor Roosevelt, advice for wives of U.S. Presidents*

Speeding

Ulysses S. Grant was the only President of the United States ever to be arrested during his term of office. He was arrested for exceeding the speed limit while driving a team of spirited horses through the streets of Washington.

No Advancement

On all but one of the few occasions when an incumbent President of the United States has declined nomination for another term, the reason for his decision has been put forth in eloquent and lofty language.

The one exception was Calvin Coolidge. When asked to elaborate on his brief announcement that he did not choose to run, his equally brief response was, "No room for advancement."

Don't They Work in the Afternoon?

A traveler in a remote tropical country stopped at a government office. He was not able to find anyone on duty except a janitor, so he asked him: "Don't they work in government offices in the afternoon?"

"Oh," the janitor replied, "it's in the morning that they don't work. In the afternoon they don't come." *Henry Kearns, Former President and Chairman, Export-Import Bank of the United States*

Sleep Like a Baby

A young man asked me how I liked being governor. I replied that I like it. When I go home at night, I sleep like a baby: sleep for an hour and then wake up and cry for an hour. *Winfield Dunn, Governor of Tennessee*

Public Office

There are two sides to every question and to hold public office you have to be for both of them.

I went to a good school where some of our foremost politicians learned their three R's—this is Ours, that is Ours, everything is Ours.

The keynote in a political campaign is the first one in the scale: "Dough."

If you don't think there is a perfect person in the world, wait until you hear a political campaign speech.

Some time science will find a way to pre-shrink a politician before election.

What a political party needs is a cash register with a good muffler on it.

155

The left and right wings of both parties are far apart, but no farther than a politician can straddle.

Our politicians discuss all the problems of the day but none of the answers.

Definitions

Isolationist: One who is against supporting the rest of the world in the style to which we are accustomed.

Diplomat: A person who permits someone else to do things the way the diplomat wants them done.

Diplomacy: The art of making someone who has just done you a small favor wish that he might have done you a greater one.

Diplomatic Agreement

When diplomats say they agree in principle, it means that in ten years the issue will be settled.

War doesn't decide which nation is right, but which one is left.

Story Has Some Merit

A horse, a cow, and a donkey were debating about which had made the greatest contribution to the war.

The horse claimed first honors, because he made it possible for the men to ride off to war and haul their cannon into position.

The cow said that were it not that she had stayed home, the civilian population would have starved within three months, and the war would have been brought to an end.

But the donkey said very boastfully, "None of you contributed as much as I, for had I not been in diplomacy at the head of the governments, there would never have been a war!"

His Estimate

Early in the Civil War, when the Union armies were suffering repeated defeats, Abraham Lincoln was discussing the war situation with his cabinet.

"How many men do you estimate are in the Confederate army?" a cabinet member asked.

"About a million and a half," Lincoln said.

"That many?" said another member. "I thought the number was considerably less."

"So did I," Lincoln said, "but every time one of our generals loses a battle, he insists that he was outnumbered three to one—and we have about 500,000 men.''

Or these words of determined faith spoken in the midst of great crises during the Civil War. In a very heated cabinet meeting one arrogant member stood and addressed Lincoln, saying, ''I hope that God will be on our side.'' To which Lincoln replied, ''I am not so much concerned about that as I am that we be on God's side.'' *Robert J. Lamont*

The Price of War

Give me the money that has been spent in war, and I will clothe every man, woman and child in an attire of which kings and queens would be proud. I will build a schoolhouse in every valley over the whole earth. I will crown every hillside with a place of worship consecrated to the gospel of peace. *Charles Sumner*

Credit

Credit: a system of buying on the lay-awake plan.

That's All

These days about the only thing you can be sure of getting for a nickel is five pennies.

Difficult Question

''There's only one thing that bugs me about this revolution bit,'' sighed one radical to another.

''And what's that?''

''What happens to our unemployment checks when we overthrow the government?''

Happy

Let us all be happy, and live within our means, even if we have to borrow the money to do it with. *Artemus Ward*

Prosperity

Prosperity is the period when it is easy to borrow money to buy things which you should be able to pay for out of your own income.

Pay As You Go

Many of us would be delighted to pay as we go, if we could only catch up with paying where we have been.

Government Expenses

The major difficulty in cutting down government expenses is that the expenses have votes.

If Uncle Sam can't balance his budget, he isn't any smarter than we are.

The government deplores the fact that the spending of many American families exceeds their income. Look who's talking!

When we look at the public debt, we're sure posterity will never be out of a job.

As a method of cutting government expenses, each cabinet head might tell how to do it in the other fellow's department.

Our foreign policy is slowly changing from an endowment policy.

We'd like to know whether the budget will be balanced by addition or subtraction.

We presume the difference between the Capitol of the United States and the capital of the United States is that the Capitol spends the capital.

We suggest Capitol Hill be called Deficit Mount.

Overextended

The patient was trying to explain his unhappiness to the psychiatrist.

"I have a son at Harvard and another son at Yale. I've bought them both brand new Cadillacs and my wife a new Buick and myself a new Italian racing car. I've a townhouse, a summer house in the country, and a beach cottage . . ."

"But all that sounds pretty good to me," interrupted the psychiatrist.

"I suppose so," said the man, "but I only make $300 a week."

Efficiency

Inflation marches on, making it possible for people in all walks of life to live in more expensive neighborhoods without even moving.

Shopping

The tot next door told it like it is: "Mommy's gone to the supermarkup."

I don't know where the money goes these days. It takes twice as much to live beyond my means as it used to.

The little girl who used to grasp a penny firmly in one hand and press her nose against the glass of a candy counter has now grown up and can be seen at the meat counter with the same look on her face as she clutches a $10 bill. *Capper's Weekly*

The Way It Goes

"Someone broke into my wife's car," said the man, "and stole $40 worth of groceries—out of the glove compartment."

Tough on Everybody

"I feel so sorry for the Joneses."

"Why?"

"With all this inflation, they can hardly keep up with themselves."

Ten years from now do you suppose we'll say a dollar went further in the good old days?

A dollar won't do as much as it used to. Do you know of anybody who does?

Definition

Inflation: Being broke with a lot of money in your pocket.

The Old Days

In the old days inflation was just something you did to a balloon or an automobile tire.

Easy to See

Little boy at fireworks display: "I want to see the cost of living sky-rocket."

Lay-Away Plan

A business executive shopping for a gift for his wife picked out a sweater in a Seattle store and then said, "Could you show me something a bit more expensive?"

The clerk said, "No, but I can put this one away and you could come back in a few days."

Tough All Around

It is tough to pay $2.50 a pound for meat, but it is still tougher if you pay less.

Sign in bakery: Because of inflation, the name of our pumpernickel bread has been changed to pumperdime.

The Money You Have

Inflation means that the money you have today won't buy as much as it would have when you didn't have any.

Statistics

Statistics prove that the best time to buy anything is a year ago.

Correct

A long-winded political speaker shouted: "What I want is reform. I want tax reform. I want judicial reform. I want high price reform. I want—I want—"

And a listener cried out: "What you want is chloroform!"

We Also See Stars

An American traveling in the Netherlands met a Hollander who, on learning the traveler's nationality, said, "Our flag is red, white, and blue, too. And when tax season approaches we begin to feel blue, and when we receive our statements we turn white, and when we pay we see red!"

"Yes," replied the American, "but in the United States we see stars as well!"

Help Available

If a person wishes to die poor today, the Internal Revenue Department is organized to help him.

Bills

Congress passes bills and the taxpayers pay them.

Going Out

I know of nothing, particularly for one who has to spend a great deal of his time in Washington in an official position, that can take the place of going out and trying again to meet Americans that are making a living and paying taxes, rather than just taking it unto themselves to spend the taxes. *Dwight Eisenhower*

Resources Gone

It looks as though the taxpayer will be the first of America's natural resources to be completely exhausted.

To offset the deficits in Federal and State governments, everything possible will finally be taxed including the citizens' credulity.

Sign at a Service Station: "We collect taxes—federal, state, local. We also sell gasoline and oil."

IRS

The Internal Revenue people know just what to give the man who has everything: an audit!

The Internal Revenue Service is a government agency that looks for people who have what it takes.

New Worry

Folks used to worry because they couldn't take it with them. In today's tax climate their only worry is whether it will last as long as they do.

In the Hole

Golf is a lot like taxes—you drive hard to get to the green and then wind up in the hole.

Anyone who thinks our country is out of the woods should visit a golf course on a weekend.

Naturally

The child swallowed a dime in a store and his frightened mother called for help. A stranger promptly seized the child by the heels, gave him a few shakes, and the coin rolled out on the floor.

The grateful mother thanked the stranger and asked, "Are you a doctor?"

"No ma'am," he replied. "I work for the Internal Revenue Service."

First Lesson

There is nothing the federal government can give you without taking it away from you first. *Dr. Edward R. Annis*

Progress

Two men were discussing taxes and the Government's use of money. Just then a school bus passed.

"See what I mean?" exclaimed one. "When I was a boy we walked three miles to school and three miles home each day. Now we spend $15,000 for a bus to pick up the children so they don't have to walk; then we spend $200,000 for a gymnasium so they can get exercise."

Isn't it hard to believe that the U.S. was founded partly to avoid taxes?

Avoid Public Debt

I place economy among the most important virtues, and public debt as the greatest of dangers to be feared. To preserve our independence we must not let our rulers load us with perpetual debt. We must make our choice between economy and liberty, or profusion and servitude. If we run into such debts we must be taxed in our meat and drink, in our necessities and in our comforts, in our labors and in our amusements. *Thomas Jefferson*

Long Ago

One historian says pre-historic man never had stooped shoulders and bowed legs. But that was before the days of government taxes.

Definition
Income tax: the fine you pay for thriving too fast.

Some Day . . .
In tax revision the emphasis should be on vision.

The Price
An optimist is one who believes shoes will cost $300 a pair by the year 2000. A pessimist believes they will cost 300 rubles.

The people in the Communist countries are finding out they can't live without eating or without buying food from the capitalist countries.

Communism assumes that it is easier to fill an empty head than an empty stomach.

A communist is a person who considers himself disloyal if he thinks for himself.

Soviet Russia is beginning to learn that her people will never have good times until a profit is not without honor in that country.

Pollution
Something's Wrong Department: Last week, fifty people picketed City Hall demanding that something be done about air pollution.
Then they got into forty-seven cars and went home.

The national parks will be visited by millions of people this year and some of the parks will be left almost intact.

Liberty
The history of liberty is a history of limitations of government power, not the increase of it. *Woodrow Wilson*

Lessons from History
It is reported that it was a Professor Tyler, of Edinburgh University back in the 18th century, who compiled the list of steps a people goes through in the course of civilization. Research does not indicate much about the man or his studies. But there can be little argument with the assumption that he had studied the history of mankind.
These are the nine steps which have come down to us as one man's assessment:
Step One: From chains of slavery, a people rises to spiritual faith.
Step Two: From spiritual faith, they generate courage.
Step Three: From courage, they forge liberty.

Step Four: From liberty comes abundance.

Step Five: From abundance arises selfishness.

Step Six: From selfishness, it is an easy progression to complacency.

Step Seven: From complacency, the next move is to apathy. (They are not the same.)

Step Eight: From apathy, a people degenerates to dependency.

Step Nine: From dependency, there is only one logical—and seemingly inevitable—move: to bondage once more.

A Grim Warning

More than a hundred years ago the British historian Lord Macaulay predicted that the United States would collapse because of the weaknesses and evils allowed to develop within it.

Here is Macaulay's dire prophecy:

"Your republic will be as fearfully plundered and laid waste by barbarians in the twentieth century as the Roman Empire was in the fifth: with this difference, that the Huns and Vandals who ravaged the Roman Empire came from without, and that your Huns and Vandals will have been engendered within your own country by your own institutions."

This grim warning was written on May 23, 1857, to a Mr. Randall, biographer of Thomas Jefferson. It appears in a pamphlet published in 1925 by the New York Public Library entitled "What Did Macaulay Say About America?"

Morality

Of the twenty-two civilizations that appeared in history, nineteen of them collapsed when they reached the moral state the U.S. is in now. *Arnold Toynbee*

Out of the Frying Pan into the Pits

Short history of civilization: When people had to cook meals outside over an open fire, they longed for an inside kitchen. When they got one, they began wishing for an outdoor barbecue pit.

Fortified Prison

There can be no such thing as Fortress America. If ever we were reduced to the isolation implied by that term we would occupy a prison, not a fortress. *Dwight D. Eisenhower*

Love Thy Neighbor

Neighborly love, in political action, means loving others, based on the brotherhood that was created with God as the Father of all. It means that the political power of any government must be considered an opportunity, not to favor individuals but to do well for all.—*John Foster Dulles, replying to a student who asked if the Secretary of State believed "Love thy neighbor" still applied to the world today*

The Challenge

The sum of the whole matter is this: Our civilization cannot survive materially unless it be redeemed spiritually. It can be saved only by the practices that spring out of that spirit. Here is the final challenge to our churches, and to everyone who fears God or loves his country. *Woodrow Wilson*

Faith

A people without faith in themselves cannot survive. *Chinese Proverb*

Humility and Patience

Humility is not one of our outstanding virtues in the United States today. Even if we tried to be humble, we would tend to be proud of it. We're like the member of a certain religious order who was asked what his order stood for, and he answered, "humility." Then he added, "At humility we beat the world." We're more apt to be known in the world for our boasting than for our humility. *Clarence W. Cranford*

How It Works

The U.S.A. is the only country where a housewife hires a woman to do her cleaning so she can do volunteer work at the day nursery where the cleaning woman leaves her child.

Sad Situation

America has become so tense and nervous it has been years since I've seen anyone sleep in church—and that is a sad situation. *Norman Vincent Peale*

Dissident Voices

There will always be dissident voices heard in the land, expressing opposition without alternatives, finding fault but never favor, perceiving gloom on every side and seeking influence without responsibility. *John F. Kennedy*

Modern Drugstore

Today's supermarket sells almost everything, but if you find automobile tires among the groceries, you're in the wrong place. That's the drugstore.

19

What Was That Again?

Good Girl

Dad noticed his 5-year-old daughter out in the backyard brushing the family dog's teeth. When he asked her what in the world she was doing, she replied quickly, "I'm brushing Scotty's teeth. But don't worry, Dad, I'll put your toothbrush back, like I always have."

Puzzled

A senator was approached in the corridor by a colleague who asked, "How was your speech at the dinner last night?"

"Well," replied the first senator, with a puzzled look, "when I sat down, the toastmaster said it was the best thing I ever did. Now I'm wondering what he meant."

He Finished First

NEIGHBOR: Where is your brother, Freddie?

FREDDIE: He's in the house playing a duet. I finished first.

Is That Clear?

Vitriolic letters arrive in Congressional offices in abundance. Most Congressmen toss them into the nearest wastebasket. Representative Morris K. Udall is showing this one, calling it a jewel of a mixed metaphor. "Of all the rats and snakes elected to office in Washington to represent the people and carry out their wishes, you rank head and shoulders beneath the lowest."

A Slip?

Former Senator Kenneth B. Keating says he doesn't know whether a Queens high school student, in a letter, made a slip of the pen or intentionally offered a subtle dig. "Please," he wrote, "send me a copy of the recent Senate Space Committee hearings. I have to write a report, and I want to read it to draw my own confusions."

Not a Great Pitcher

I don't want to leave you or my athletic career with the idea that I was just a one-sport athlete. I also pitched some for the baseball team. I am not a great pitcher, and I remember one time one of my last turns on the mound for our college team, and we were having a little trouble. You know how the manager will do when the pitcher is in a little trouble. He will walk out to the mound. He will take the ball and give it to some other joker so he can pitch.

That is what this guy did. He called time out. He comes out to where I am standing on the mound, and he reaches for that ball.

I jerked it back. I said, "Now, just a minute. You see that next batter coming up over there? Last time he was up, I struck him out."

He looked at me and he said, "Heck, yes, but we are still in the same inning."—*Robert Delvaney, Athletic Director of the University of Nebraska*

Plain English

A woman noticed a beautiful display of dried flowers in a shop window. She asked the shopkeeper how he had preserved the flowers so nicely.

"You just put 'em in a box with cornmeal and borax and barium," he drawled.

The woman was sure she could get cornmeal and borax and she thought her son would have some barium in a chemistry set.

Before she left the shop she checked again just to make sure. "Now I use equal parts of cornmeal and borax and barium. Right?"

"Yes, ma'am," answered the shopkeeper. "That's all there is to it. Just be sure you don't barium too deep."

Laughter

An optimist laughs to forget; a pessimist forgets to laugh.

Way Back Then

Archeologist to colleague studying ancient stone tablet: "Well, roughly translated, it says, 'Don't fold, spindle, or mutilate.' "

Suspicious

Seeing an old typewriter in a Sussex junk shop, a correspondent went in to inquire about its condition and price.

"Only one man has asked about it," the proprietor said frankly, "and I think he was a Communist. He typed out something to the effect that it was time for all good men to come to the aid of the party." *Peter Peterborough, Daily Telegraph, London*

Say That Again

GROCER: You want a pound of ochre? You mean red ochre for mixing with paint?

LITTLE BOY: No. Tabby ochre. Mom wants to make a pudding out of it.

False Advertising

SON: That man wasn't a painless dentist like he advertised.

FATHER: Why? Did he hurt you?

SON: No, but he yelled when I bit his thumb, just like the other dentist.

Bad Time

He had a miserable time at the party. In fact, he was so glad to get home, he was glad he went.

A Hard Winter

During last winter's violent snowstorms, one Red Cross rescue team was carried by helicopter to within a mile of a mountain cabin all but covered by deep snowdrifts.

The rescuers struggled on foot through the deep drifts and finally arrived at the cabin, where they shoveled away enough snow to clear the door. They knocked, and when their summons was answered by a mountaineer, one rescuer said, "We're from the Red Cross."

"Well," said the mountaineer, scratching his head, "It's been a right tough winter, and I don't see as how we can give anything this year."

Just So He Is Healthy

"He's the very image of me!" exclaimed the proud new father.

"Well, Joe," gently replied his friend, "I wouldn't worry about it, so long as he's healthy."

How's That?

The president of the men's club was addressing the assembled membership: "In most organizations," he said, "half the members do all the work and the other half do nothing. I am happy to say that in this club, we do the exact opposite."

Both Go Back

"This table," said an aristocratic lady, "goes back to Louis the Fourteenth."

"You don't have a thing on me," replied her maid. "My whole dining room set goes back to Sears on the thirteenth."

Of Course

The boastful young man had the floor. "Yes," he declared, "my family can trace its ancestry back to William the Conqueror."

"I suppose," snapped a listener, "you'll be telling us that your ancestors were in Noah's Ark."

"Certainly not," said the boaster; "my people owned a boat of their own."

Say That Again
The farmer was digging ditches when his shovel handle broke, so he drove to a nearby store for a replacement. The owner spent twenty minutes rummaging through his storeroom. At last he found a handle that matched the broken one.

"How much?" asked the man.

"It's $2.98 but I can't sell it," replied the storekeeper.

"Why not?"

"Well, this is the only one I have in stock and I have to keep it in case somebody needs one."

Honest
MAGICIAN (*to small boy called up on stage to assist*): Now, my boy, you've never seen me before, have you?

SMALL BOY: No, Daddy.

It Takes Patience
Some jobs have to be put off dozens of times before they completely slip your mind.

Don't We All
Every time I think of how humble I am, I feel so proud.

Bad Cold
A Martian landed in Las Vegas and passed by a slot machine that whirred noisily, then disgorged a jackpot of silver dollars. The Martian said to the machine: "You're foolish not to stay home with a cold like that." *Charles Winick, Newsweek*

Mistakes
A man seldom makes the same mistake twice. Generally, it's three times or more.

By making the same mistake over and over again, one at least learns to do one thing wrong well.

Practical
A practical man is a man who practices the errors of his forefathers. *Benjamin Disraeli*

Definition?
Brain: The apparatus with which we think we think.

Heart of Gold
Don't forget that people judge you by your actions, not your intentions.

You may have a heart of gold, but so does a hard-boiled egg.

Time to Diet

An acquaintance asked Jackie Gleason whether he wasn't putting on weight. "All I can tell you," said Gleason, "is that the other day I got on a weighing machine that stamps your weight on a card. When the card came out it said, 'Come back in ten minutes—alone.' "

Good Advice

The brakes on the family car failed while the wife was driving. "What shall I do?" she asked, terrified.

Her quick-witted husband's reply was, "Hit something cheap."

Women and Girls

A ten-year-old boy's essay on women: "A rose is a rose, is a rose, is a rose . . . and it's the same way with girls."

It Makes a Difference

The new dishwasher didn't work well, and the housewife called the company that had installed it. An inspector came out, looked things over and said: "Well, the trouble is that it's connected to the cold water instead of the hot." He called the plumber to come back.

The plumber was pretty grumpy at the idea he should be blamed. "Sure," he said, "I know the hot water is on the left—but I was working on the pipes from the other side."

That's Different

The retiring usher was instructing his youthful successor in the details of his office. "And remember, my boy, that we have nothing but good, kind Christians in this church—until you try to put someone else in their pew."

It's Easy

A golf professional, hired by a big department store to give golf lessons, was approached by two women.

"Do you wish to learn to play golf, madam?" he asked one.

"Oh, no," she said, "it's my friend who wants to learn. I learned yesterday."

Dinner Call

A correspondent recalls that he used to pass a sea scout camp near a beach where the porpoises were so friendly they swam into shore at dinner time.

"The habit became so consistent," writes Mr. Geidel, "that the chef used to announce dinner by yelling: 'Dinner! For all in tents—and porpoises.' " *John G. Fuller, Saturday Review*

Mother May Be Right

MOTHER: I don't think the man upstairs likes Johnnie to play on his drum.

FATHER: Why?

MOTHER: Well, this afternoon he gave Johnnie a knife and asked him if he knew what was inside the drum.

Most Men

Most men are ready to blow their own horns before the silence becomes unbearable.

Horse Sense

Horse sense is what keeps a horse from betting on a man.

I Didn't Cry

It hurt, but I didn't cry, mother; I just clouded up.

Most Happy Fellow

The fellow who is always happy is probably too lazy to complain.

Letter to the Editor

A Scot wrote to the editor of a magazine saying if he didn't stop publishing Scottish jokes, he'd quit borrowing the magazine.

Living It Up

The fellow who lives it up often has trouble trying to live it down.

Flattery

Flattery is the one thing that will turn even a head on a stiff neck.

Like a Gentleman

"Where's Pete lately?"

"Haven't you heard? He got three years for stealing a car."

"What did he steal a car for? Why didn't he just buy it and not pay for it, like a gentleman?"

Quartet

A quartet is where all four think the other three can't sing.

Could Be an Economist

Sir Winston Churchill, asked what were the qualifications essential for a politician, replied:

"The ability to foretell what will happen tomorrow, next month and next year—and to explain afterwards why it didn't happen."

Naturally

A little lad at the zoo wanted to know why the giraffe had such a long neck.

"Well," said the keeper, "the giraffe's head is so far from his body that a long neck is absolutely necessary."

Not Cheap

A nearsighted old lady had spent a long time in the curiosity shop. "What is that ugly oriental figure in the corner worth?" she asked at last.

"About fifty thousand," whispered the horrified salesman. "That's the proprietor."

Probably

They say that a certain young man married a girl because her rich uncle left her a million dollars. We believe he would have married her no matter who left it to her.

Good Reason

INSTALLMENT COLLECTOR: See here, you've never made a single payment on your piano.

KENNY: Well, the company advertises "Pay As You Play."

COLLECTOR: What has that to do with it?

KENNY: I don't play.

Pleasure

To take the most pleasure out of life you can't put too much pleasure in.

Breeding

A well-bred person is one who conceals his own high esteem of himself.

Pessimist

A pessimist is an optimist who thought he could buy something for a dollar.

Smart Bird

A sailor went to an auction sale, where the auctioneer was offering a parrot. He bid $5. Someone said $10, and the sailor bid $15. Again someone bid $25, and the sailor bid $40, and he finally got the bird.

As he walked out, he said to the auctioneer, "That's a big price to pay for a parrot. Can he talk?"

The auctioneer replied, "You ought to know. He's the one that was bidding against you."

He Hates It

Small boy, at the guest table: "No, I don't like spinach, and I'm glad I don't like it, for if I did, I'd eat it, and I hate the stuff!''

Egotism
Egotism is the ability to see things in yourself that others cannot see.

Anesthetics
Some of the stuff that comes to TV and the radio through the ether makes any other anesthetic look weak.

Fads
A fad is something that goes in one era and out the other.

Last Stop
On a little service station away out on the edge of a western desert, there hangs a shingle bearing this strange legend: ''Don't ask us for information. If we knew anything we wouldn't be here.''

Professional Women
We never quite understand the words ''professional women.'' Are there amateurs?

20

Definitions Not in Mr. Webster's Dictionary

Absolutely positive—Being completely mistaken at the top of your voice.

Acquaintance—A degree of friendship called slight when its object is poor or obscure, and intimate when he is rich or famous. *Ambrose Bierce*

Admiration—Our polite recognition of another man's resemblance to ourselves. *Ambrose Bierce*

Adolescent—A youngster who is old enough to dress himself, if he could just remember where he dropped his clothes.

Alarm Clock—A mechanism used to scare the daylights into you.

Albany—A city where the Late Late show starts at 6:30 P.M.

Appendix—What you have out before the doctor decides it's your gall bladder.

Arthritis—Twinges in the hinges.

Auction—A place where, if you aren't careful, you'll get something for nodding.

Balanced Diet—What you eat at a buffet supper.

Bolt and a Nut

High school examination question: "Define a bolt and nut, and explain the difference."

One girl wrote: "A bolt is a thing like a stick of hard metal, such as iron, with a square bunch on one end and a lot of scratching wound around the other end. A nut is similar to the bolt only just the opposite, being a hole in a little chunk of iron sawed off short, with wrinkles around the inside of the hole."

The startled professor marked that one with an "A." *Capper's Weekly*

Bore—A person who talks when you wish him to listen. *Ambrose Bierce*

Bore—A fellow who opens his mouth and puts his feats in it.

Burglar—A person who will work all hours of the night to get out of life what he didn't put in.

Church choir—Twenty-four people who think the other 23 can't sing very well.

College professor—Someone who talks in other people's sleep. *Bergen Evans*

Conceit—A queer disease. It makes everyone sick except the fellow who has it.

Conscience is that still, small voice that tells you what other people should do.

A **conservative** is a statesman who is enamored of existing evils, as distinguished from the liberal who wishes to replace them with others. *Ambrose Bierce*

Cynic—A person who believes other people are as bad as he is.

Diet—Something to take the starch out of you.

Duty—The thing you recognize in time to avoid it.

Egotist—A person who never goes around talking about other people.

Egotist—A person who is always blowing his knows.

Elephant—A mouse put together on a cost-plus basis.

Fisherman—A guy who thinks a fish should bite on a fancy lure just because he did.

Golf

Ball—A sphere made of rubber bands wound up about half as tensely as the man trying to hit it.

Course—A mirage; looks smooth, lush and grassy, but actually sand and the five Great Lakes.

Drive—An afternoon spin which, though scenic, is made up of dense forest, acres of heavily wooded areas.

Fairway—The well-kept and seldom used portion of a golf course.

Fore—Golfing equivalent of the air raid siren (fall flat, face down, cover back of neck with hands).

Flag—Beacon to a rallying point where members of a foursome meet every twenty minutes or so to exchange alibis.

Hazard—Man-made difficulties, consisting of equal parts of sand, water, profanity and ulcers.

Hook—An unexpected detour.

Par—Mathematical perfection, usually attained with a soft pencil and not-so-soft conscience.

Chicago Rotary Club

Gossip—The art of saying nothing in a way that leaves nothing unsaid.

Government Bureau—Where the taxpayer's shirt is kept.

Gravitation—What happens to a man's socks without garters.

Grouch—A fellow who has sized himself up and is sore about it.

Happiness—Watching a snowplow completely cover a police car.

Happiness for toddlers—Three friends in a sandbox.

Historian—A person who tells it like it was.

Home—A tax shelter.

Information—Organized ignorance.

Insomnia—What a person has when he lies awake all night for an hour.

Instant—The length of time it takes a supermarket cash register to reach $10.

Instant Pizza—Pizza that makes you sick at once instead of at 3 A.M.

Loneliness—The feeling you have when you are without money among relatives.

Man—An inconsistent animal who insists on hotel service at home.

Miser—A person who lets the world go buy.

Moderate—A fellow who makes enemies left and right.

Neurotic—A person who worries about things that didn't happen in the past, instead of worrying about something that won't happen in the future, like normal people.

Patience—The ability to count down before blasting off.

Patience—What you have when you don't know what to do next.

Patience may be simply the inability to make a decision.

Pessimist—A person who only laughs when he hears a definition of an optimist.

Philosopher—A person who confuses you sufficiently to make you believe he knows what he is talking about.

Philosopher—A person who makes ignorance sound profound.

Picnics—Occasions when people have their outings, and insects their innings.

Plenty—The difference between socialism and private enterprise.

Poise—The art of raising the eyebrows instead of the roof.

Poise—The ability to talk fluently while the other fellow is paying the check.

Practical Nurse—One who falls in love with a rich patient.

Of Course
"Dad, what do pro and con mean?"
"Well, son, pro is your convincing, unalterable argument, and con is the other fellow's contemptible drivel."

176

Psychiatrist—A fellow who makes you squeal on yourself.

Rabbit—A little animal that grows the fur the other animals get credit for when it is made into a lady's coat.

Sardines—Little fish that crawl into a can, lock themselves up, and leave the key outside.

Secret—Something that is hushed about from place to place.

Ship of State—A splendid vessel, but badly overloaded with stowaways in the form of bureaucrats.

Small town—A place where they are proud of their traffic congestion.

Summer—The season of the year which bugs us!

Summer camp counselor—A person who used to think he liked children.

Tact—Changing the subject without changing your mind.

Teamwork—When a family is fighting to keep the wolf away from the door, and the stork slips down the chimney.

Teenager—A person who reaches for a chair when answering the phone.

Tourist—A person who travels a thousand miles to get a snapshot of himself standing beside his car.

Traffic light—A trick to get pedestrians halfway across the street.

Traitor—Any California doctor advising a change of climate for his patients.

Is That Clear?

"Do you want a room with a tub or a shower?" the clerk asked.
"What's the difference?" the caller replied.
"Well," came the patient response, "with a tub, you sit down."

A **vacuum** is nothing shut up in a box.

Waiter—A person whose chief business is hiding out.

21

Verses Shakespeare Didn't Write

It Couldn't
They told me it couldn't be done. But I grinned and went right to it. I tackled the job that couldn't be done. And, you know, I couldn't do it!

Right of Way
To every person comes his day, so calmly wait your chance; pedestrians have the right of way when in an ambulance.

You Can Buy Loyalty
You can't buy loyalty, they say. I bought it though, the other day. You can't buy friendship tried and true. Well, just the same, I bought that, too.

I made my bid, and on the spot bought love and faith and a whole job lot of happiness; so all in all the total price was pretty small.

I bought a simple, trusting heart that gave devotion from the start. If you think these things are not for sale, buy a brown-eyed pup with a wagging tail!

By Dose
It doesn't breathe, it doesn't smell, it doesn't feel so very well. I am discouraged with by dose, the only thing it does is blows.

Here Today — Gone Tomorrow
This one bold fact I face with sorrow: my hair today is gone tomorrow.

Babies haven't any hair; old men's heads are just as bare; between the cradle and the grave lie just a haircut and a shave.

The Night Before
'Tis the night before payday, and all through my jeans I've hunted in vain for the ways and the means. Not a quarter is stirring, not even a bit; the green backs have left me, the pennies have quit.

Forward, turn forward, O Time, in thy flight, and make it tomorrow just for tonight! *Evans Echoes*

178

I Get There

I think that I shall never see a driver half as dumb as me; a driver who can't park his own within the parking meter zone; who waits at intersections, shy, till all the other cars go by; who timidly moves on, and then— that lousy light goes red again.

But still I've never killed a guy, or crippled any passerby. I move along with slow advance and never take just one more chance. And if I seem slow to arrive, at least I turn up still alive.

It's Not for Me

Here's to him who early rises and goes through his exercises; wakens from his tranquil sleep, exhales slowly, inhales deep; who always steps right out of bed, stretching arms above his head; bending over, touching toes. I am never one of those. Mornings, I'm too hot or cold; and other times, I'm just too old.

Dieting

Hey, diddle, diddle, I'm watching my middle, and hoping to whittle it soon; but eating's such fun, I may not get it done 'til my dish runs away with my spoon.

Counting Sheep

I'm practically dead from lack of sleep and from counting erratic sheep; and one sheep's left that should have gone, but his tail got caught in the crack of dawn.

Score One for Mom

My son has trimmed his dangling locks, he's cut and let them fall. And all because of what he termed "The cruelest words of all."

So now he's past the long-hair stage; and though I'm no contriver, it did me good to hear him called, "A crazy woman driver."

Commuter

One who spends his life, in riding to and from his wife; a man who shaves and takes a train, and then rides back to shave again.

Weather

Whether it rain or whether it snow, we shall have weather, whether or no. And whether we smile or whether we fuss, the weather won't alter a bit for us.

So when it's foggy, we won't complain; and when it's rainy we'll let it rain; and when the weather is clear and fine and old Sol's shining, we'll let him shine!

"Whether it's cool or whether it's hot, we shall have weather, whether or not." But though I'm cheerful as I can be, I like to feel that I'm wholly free to kick and growl if I do not like the kind of weather I chance to strike. Over the climate I've no dominion—but, I'm entitled to my opinion!

It's Spring

"It's spring," said the poet. His wife said, "I know it; and this year I want to remind you, it's time to clean house, and you, my dear spouse, better stay around where I can find you!" *Nuggets*

Then and Now

When Grandpa went past seventy, he called it "borrowed time." He thanked the Lord for mercy and thought it very fine.

Now his grandson passes ninety, but it isn't very funny; he'll never live on "borrowed time," but does on borrowed money.

Home of the Freeway

The man who said "Go West" never had to figure out how to do it on a cloverleaf intersection. Or, as a modern day patriot once put it: "Lane borders lane and you haven't much leeway—in the land of the brave and the home of the freeway."

Why?

Why must I, when courting sleep, see bright ideas instead of sheep? Why, when upon my couch I lie, do epic thoughts come trooping by? And why when I am upright, pray, do these keen gems just fade away?

Vacationer's Prayer

Dear Lord, when Gabriel blows his blast, and I come home to rest at last, don't measure me for harp or wings; just let me have instead these things: some tackle, and a rod and reel; a pair of waders and a creel; a gushing, lovely glacier stream, and a placid lake by which to dream; an angel pal with whom to angle; magic lines that will not tangle; and permission, Lord, with fingers crossed, to stretch the truth of the fish I lost.

Too True

Most folks love to watch for mail, it brings them countless thrills; but all we ever seem to get is loads of unpaid bills.

Prize Growl

It's easy enough to be grouchy, when things aren't coming your way, but the prize old growl is the man who can howl when everything's going okay.

One Talent

I have no voice for singing; I cannot make a speech; I have no gift for music, I know I cannot teach.

I am no good at leading; I cannot "organize," and anything I write would never win a prize.

It seems my only talent is neither big nor rare—just to listen and encourage, and to fill a vacant chair.

Careful

I'm careful of the words I say; I keep them soft and sweet. I never know from day to day which ones I'll have to eat.

Sit Alone and Think

It's a busy world we live in; we get caught up in the race. And sometimes our sense of values, slips a little out of place. It's a good thing to pull over to the roadside now and then, and get our thinking straightened out before we start again.

Didn't Kilmer Play Golf?

I think that I shall never see my ball beneath a spreading tree, whose roots give me a dreadful lie, whose branches strike me in the eye, whose leaves obliterate the view, whose trunk prevents a follow-through. I'll never see a tree, I swear, and not wish it were elsewhere.

Conserve Gas

Lock up your auto in the old garage, and smile, smile, smile. Ride to your business in a bus or barge, or walk mile after mile. What's the use of worrying? It never was worth while, so lock up your auto in the old garage, and smile, smile, smile.

Advice

A doctor fell into a well, and broke his collarbone. A doctor should attend the sick, and leave the well alone. *School Life*

What's Botany?

There should be no monotony in studying your botany. It helps to train and spur the brain—unless you haven't gotany.

It teaches you—does botany—to know the plants and spotany, and learn just why they live and die, in case you plant or potany.

You learn from reading botany of woolly plants and cottony that grow on earth, and what they're worth, and why some spots have notany.

You sketch the plants in botany; you learn to chart and plotany, like corn or oats. You jot down notes—if you know how to jotany.

Your time, if you'll allotany, will teach you how and whatany old plants or trees can do or be. And that's the use of botany! *Berton Braley in B-L-S Friendly Chat*

Good Reason

I want my peas with honey, and, like I tell my wife, they do taste kind of funny, but it keeps them on the knife.

The Way to Be Happy

If you wish to be happy, we'll tell you the way: don't live tomorrow till you've lived today.

If You Belong

Are you an active member, the kind that would be missed? Or are you just contented that your name is on the list? Do you attend the meetings, and mingle with the flock, or do you stay at home and criticize and knock? Do you take an active part to help the work along, or are you satisfied to be the kind that "just belong"?

Letter to Santa

Dear Santa: This coming Christmas Eve,
Will you be kind enough to leave,
Besides the toys you have for me,
Some duplicates for Dad, that he
May tinker with his own, and play
As fathers will on Christmas Day?
Then I, for once, won't have to wait
For days and days to celebrate.

Sunshine Magazine

The Tongue in Verse

"The boneless tongue, so small and weak, can crush and kill," declares the Greek.

"The tongue destroys a greater horde," the Turk asserts, "than does the sword."

The Persian proverb wisely saith, "A lengthy tongue, an early death." Or sometimes takes this form instead: "Don't let your tongue cut off your head."

"The tongue can speak a word whose speed," say the Chinese, "out-strips the steed."

While Arab sages this impart: "The tongue's great storehouse is the heart."

From Hebrew wit the maxim sprung, "Though feet should slip, ne'er let the tongue."

The sacred writer crowns the whole: "Who keeps his tongue doth keep his soul."

22

Success

Thanks

Let us be thankful for the fools. But for them the rest of us could not succeed. *Mark Twain*

How He Got There

When you see a turtle on top of a fence post, you know he didn't get there by himself. *Robert J. Lamont*

A Fast Outfield

Lefty Gomez asked the secret of his remarkable World Series pitching record. "Clean living and a fast outfield," was the reply. No man ever succeeds by himself. *Robert W. Youngs, Christian Herald*

Surprise

Back of every achievement is a proud wife and a surprised mother-in-law. *Brooks Hays*

It's Not Difficult

A millionaire's wife told a reporter: "It's not true that I married a millionaire. I made him one myself."

"What was he before you married him?" asked the reporter.

"A multimillionaire."

Golf

Only a few men owe their success to golf. Most of them owe their golf to success.

The First Step

The man who removes a mountain begins by carrying away small stones. *Chinese Proverb*

Conscience

The person who has the approval of his own conscience has a powerful ally.

Worth Remembering

With the single exception of clapping hands, the sweetest sound a mortal ever hears is that of his own name. It assures him that he is important enough to be recognized and remembered. And that is the first secret of success. *Robert Quillen*

Only for an Acrobat

Keep your head level, both feet on the ground, your back to the wall, your shoulder to the wheel, and your nose to the grindstone. You will get along.

Bringing Home the Bacon

It generally helps you to bring home the bacon if you pass out a little applesauce.

Accomplishment

Keep on going and the chances are you will stumble on something, perhaps when you are least expecting it. I have never heard of anyone stumbling on something sitting down. *Charles F. Kettering*

Learned-Useful-Valiant

It is not what we read, but what we remember, that makes us learned. It is not what we intend, but what we do, that makes us useful. It is not a few faint wishes, but a lifelong struggle, that makes us valiant. *Henry Ward Beecher*

Thoughts for the Day

I got a postcard addressed to the Very Rev. Archbishop Bruce Larson, Inc. On the other side in a big, red scrawl with a felt tip pen the sender wrote, "Thought for the day! If you plan to swallow a frog, it is best not to look at it too long. If you have a number of frogs to swallow, swallow the big one first. Signed, Yours till the water freezes in the pail, George." *Bruce Larson*

Greatness is a two-faced coin—and its reverse is humility.

The tortoise may win from the hare that falls asleep in the race, but the tortoise can't count on every hare falling asleep.

Accomplishment

To accomplish great things, we must not only act but also dream, not only plan but also believe. *Anatole France*

You may be on the right track, but if you just sit there, you'll be run over.

Believing

"One can't believe impossible things." "I daresay you haven't had much practice," said the Queen. "When I was your age, I always did it for half-an-hour a day. Why, sometimes I've believed as many as six impossible things before breakfast." *Lewis Carroll*

Forget

Blessed are those who forget, for they thus surmount even their mistakes. *Friedrich Nietzsche*

Wise Advice

To a young man learning to perform on the flying trapeze a veteran circus performer once said: "Throw your heart over the bars and your body will follow." In every field of endeavor those who put their hearts in their work are the real successes.

There aren't any hard-and-fast rules for getting ahead in the world—just hard ones.

Discontent

Restlessness is discontent—and discontent is the first necessity of progress. Show me a thoroughly satisfied man, and I will show you a failure. *Thomas A. Edison*

How to Succeed

Hitch your wagon to a star, put your shoulder to the wheel, keep your ear to the ground and watch the handwriting on the wall.

One way to the top is to go to the bottom of everything.

Personality often goes a long way as a substitute for ability.

Ever notice how some folks who stop to think never start again?

If you want a place in the sun, you must expect to get blistered.

He Listens

During his years as football coach at the University of Illinois, Bob Zuppke taught his boys to play hard.

One day, during a practice session, an assistant said to him: "We are going to show the boys how to tackle. Do you want to watch?"

Zuppke shook his head. "I never watch tackles," he said. "I listen for them."

The difference between a wise guy and a wise man is plenty.

A Successful Coach

I have been labeled at times as a successful coach. Long ago I heard the definition of a successful coach. A successful coach is a coach who, when being run out of town by an angry mob of alumni, can make it appear as if he is leading a parade. *Robert Delvaney, Athletic Director of the University of Nebraska, before the Executives Club of Chicago*

The Uneasy Life

The newly rich manufacturer and his wife were having difficulty adjusting to a life of elegance. After the first dinner in their new 25-room mansion, the husband turned to his wife and asked, "Shall we have our after-dinner coffee in the library?"

"It's too late," she replied. "The library closes at six."

Sad

The late Henry Ford in an interview with a young reporter was asked just what he felt were the disadvantages of great wealth. "Well," replied Mr. Ford, sadly, "for me it was when Mrs. Ford quit cooking."

Advantage

One advantage a poor man has is that he never leaves his car keys in his other pants.

Not Worth It

If someone should offer to give you a billion dollars in one dollar bills, if you would count it, would you accept it? Well, it would take you about sixty years, eight hours per day, three hundred and sixty-five days in the year to do the job. And perhaps before you were half through you would be broken in health.

Shame

It's a shame that when success turns a person's head it does not also wring his neck just a little.

Necessary Misfortune

Success is the necessary misfortune of life, but it is only to the very unfortunate that it comes early. *Anthony Trollope*

Prescription

Success is a poison that should only be taken late in life and then only in small doses. *Anthony Trollope*

Prosperity

Most people can't stand prosperity, but then most people don't have to.

Goals

Success is the brand on the brow of the man who aimed too low. *John Masefield*

Public Office

As some of the legislators told of frustration in trying to get things done, Mr. Unruh commented that it always surprised him that so many good men and women kept at it. It reminded him of the fellow who came to a small Southern town and decided to look up an old college chum who had been named Mayor.

It being Saturday afternoon, he asked at a gas station where he might find Mayor Jones, and was told, "That no good so and so? He's probably off fishing, just like every other day." An inquiry at a drugstore got the answer, "That jerk. I wouldn't tell you if I knew." After several more attempts got similarly hostile answers, he decided to go by City Hall on the chance someone might be there who could direct him to his friend's house. The building was almost deserted, but there in the mayor's office, hard at work, was his old friend.

After a few pleasantries, the out-of-towner asked why his friend wanted a job that kept him working on a lovely Saturday afternoon—was it the high salary? "Oh, no," the mayor replied, "there's no pay at all." Well, then, the graft—paving contracts and the like? No, all city contracts were let by competitive bidding. Perhaps the mayor controlled a lot of patronage? No, all the jobs were civil service.

"Why in the world then," demanded the out-of-towner, "do you take a job like this?"

Replied the mayor, "For the prestige, of course."

*   *   *

This prompted West Virginia State Representative Charles Cline to recall the colleague who opened a speech by asking the press not to report his remarks. "I wouldn't want my old mother to know I'm in the legislature," the member explained. "She thinks I'm in prison." *From a column by Alan L. Otten in the Wall Street Journal*

Upper Class

An upper-class neighborhood is one in which you can sit in the yard in your shorts but not in your undershirt.

Money

Money never makes a fool of a man, but it may expose the fool in him.

Trouble Can Be Opportunity

Trouble and opportunity often look so much alike that a person can never be sure which one is really knocking on the door. Sometimes what looks like opportunity turns out to be nothing but trouble, and what looks like trouble proves to be opportunity.

By 1849, for instance, Nathaniel Hawthorne had already published considerable work, but none of it established his position in the field of letters. Along with his writing he also held at different times several government posts, including being U.S. consul, Liverpool, England.

What looked like trouble came in 1849 when Hawthorne lost his position as surveyor at the customhouse. But in the year that followed he wrote *The Scarlet Letter*. This book immediately gave him a distinctive and permanent place in American literature.

The loss of a job looked like trouble, but in the end it proved to be opportunity. *Sunshine Magazine*

Opportunity
They do me wrong
who say I come no more
When once I knock
and fail to find you in;
For every day
I stand outside your door,
And bid you wake,
and rise to fight and win.

Walter Malone

Some men rise to the occasion, while others merely go up in the air.

Opportunities drop in your lap if you have your lap where opportunities drop. *Herbert V. Prochnow*

Opportunity doesn't knock these days; it rings the phone and asks a silly question.

Some persons not only expect opportunity to knock, but they also want it to break the door down.

Impossible
In November, 1837, Dionysius Lardner, distinguished British physicist, demonstrated mathematically and irrefutably, with equations nobody could question, that it was impossible to build a steamship capable of non-stop voyage to New York. Printed copies of his lecture proving this "fact" arrived in Manhattan on April 24, 1838, aboard the steamer Sirius, first to cross the Atlantic entirely under steam.

Robert Fulton's Confidence
When someone is convinced that things can't be done, he will cling to

that conviction in the face of the most obvious contradiction. At the time that Robert Fulton gave the first public demonstration of his steamboat, one of those "can't be done" fellows stood in the crowd along the shore repeating, "He can't start her." Suddenly there was a belch of steam and smoke and the steamboat began slowly to move. Startled, the man stared for a moment and then began to chant, "He can't stop her." *Sunshine Magazine*

The Most Remarkable

Several years ago an athlete named Charles Zimmy was determined to achieve fame as a long-distance swimmer. After intensive training he began making sports headlines with his incredible aquatic performances.

Zimmy first established an endurance record by swimming for 80 consecutive hours. Next he upped his mark by logging 100 continuous hours near Honolulu.

Still not satisfied, Charles announced that he would attempt to swim the Hudson River from Albany to New York City. Overcoming fatigue, hunger and sleepiness, he startled the skeptical nation by completing the 147-mile trip nonstop!

Of all long-distance swimmers, Zimmy still ranks as the most remarkable because he had no legs. *The Christian Athlete*

To Do It Now

In science and engineering, young men have early dedicated their lives to the pursuit of knowledge. James Watt at the age of twenty-four started work on the steam engine, Edison at twenty-six was already famous, Bell would go on and patent the telephone at twenty-nine, Westinghouse invented the air brakes at twenty-two, Einstein at twenty-six propounded the theory of relativity and Pasteur at twenty-five revolutionized chemistry. Should I go on? These men are the now people, they wanted to be with it, to press on now to the things which challenge. *Robert J. Lamont*

Don't Give Up

BILL: Have you ever realized any of your childhood hopes?

PETE: Yes, when mother used to comb my hair, I often wished I didn't have any.

Quick Wit

It is said that Ruth Bryan, daughter of William Jennings Bryan, started for school one morning and after a desperate run for a bus finally succeeded in catching it.

"Well," she said, as she took her seat, "I'm glad there is one member of the family who can run for something and get it."

Monument

Monuments! What are they? The very pyramids have forgotten their builders, or to whom they were dedicated. Deeds, not stones, are the true monuments of the great. *John Lothrop Motley*

True Success

To laugh often and love much
To win the respect of intelligent persons and the affection of children
To earn the approbation of honest critics and endure the betrayal of false friends
To appreciate beauty
To find the best in others
To give one's self
To leave the world a bit better, whether by a healthy child, a garden patch or a redeemed social condition
To have played and laughed with enthusiasm and sung with exultation
To know even one life has breathed easier because you have lived—
This is to have succeeded.

Ralph Waldo Emerson

Believe It or Not

Out of the storehouse of a man's mind come the raw materials which will build his castle or his hovel. A few years ago a young sports cartoonist on *The New York Globe* was earning $22.50 a week and glad to get it. Along came the boss with a demand for something out of the ordinary in sports comics. The cartoonist dug into his memory storehouse. He remembered the feat of J. J. Darby, an Englishman who jumped backwards 13 feet with weights in his hands. He thought of Pauliquen, the Parisian, who stayed under water 6 minutes and 29 seconds.

He assembled these and several similar ideas in a three-column cartoon, and because he could not think of a definite title, he called the drawing, "Believe It Or Not." Those four words, and the idea behind them, paid Robert L. Ripley a million-a-year dividends.

Abraham Lincoln

It is the struggle, the striving and the testing which makes success really worthwhile. Do you realize that in twenty-eight years of constant striving Abraham Lincoln was able to achieve only one victory of any consequence? Here in all too brief a word is a chronological account of Lincoln's struggle to find fulfillment and happiness. When he was twenty-three years old—that would have been in 1832—he was a partner in a little store. Because of the duplicity of his partner, the business ended in bankruptcy with a sheriff's sign on the door. In trying to rebuild his life, he ran for the legislature in 1832 only to fail in the election. In 1833 he failed in business

190

again. His partner was drunk most of the time. In the midst of liquidation, his partner died and Lincoln assumed responsibility for all the debt. He was thirty-nine years of age when the last of the indebtedness was paid. In the meantime, he took a job as a surveyor, only to have his creditors levy on his instruments and horse, without which he could not continue.

In 1834, Lincoln was elected to the legislature but within a few months his sweetheart died. His biographers say, "His heart followed her to the grave." The following year he had a nervous breakdown and lived on the verge of insanity. His suicidal tendencies were so great that he never even dared to carry a pocket knife. Lincoln was taken to the home of his parents some 300 miles away to recuperate. Once again he tried to take the shattered hopes of his life and put them together. He ran for Speaker of the State House and lost. In 1843, he ran for nomination for Congress and was resoundingly defeated.

In 1846, he was finally elected to Congress, but after a two-year term his constituents refused to re-elect him. He tried another way of earning a living as a land officer, and was rejected for that office in 1849. He ran for the Senate in 1854 and when the state nominating convention was split along party lines, Lincoln stepped aside for another candidate. He was defeated for nomination as Vice President in the convention of 1856. He tried for the Senate again in 1858. Out of this contest came the famous Lincoln-Douglas debates. Lincoln was overwhelmingly defeated. Finally, in 1860, Abraham Lincoln was elected President. In almost thirty years of trying, he knew practically nothing of success nor victory. But he discovered resources deep within himself and in God which produced that wonderful combination of "strength and tenderness" that was so deeply needed in the Presidency. Ultimately he was God's man in God's time and for God's purpose. *Robert J. Lamont*

Failure

The 15-year old youngster stood sheepishly before the headmaster of a Munich school who was "reading the riot act" to him. The boy was soundly censured for lack of interest in his studies and was asked to leave school. "Your presence in the class destroys the respect of the students," the headmaster said. The youngster took an examination to enter the Swiss Federal Polytechnic School in Zurich, but failed to pass. He entered another school, finished his training, and then applied for an assistantship at the Polytechnic. Again he was rejected. He finally secured a position as a tutor for boys in a boarding house, but soon was fired. Finally, he managed to obtain a job in the patent office in Bern. The man who compiled this string of failures was none other than the great teacher and mathematician Albert Einstein. *Joseph Hutnyan*

23

I'll Take the High Road

Amen

An old minister was seeking to inspire his somewhat apathetic audience. Said he: "This church must get up and walk."

"Amen," exclaimed a pious brother, "let her walk!"

"This church," added the minister, "must run."

"Amen, let her run," said the saintly man.

"More than that," shouted the preacher, encouraged by the response, "this church must fly."

"Amen," ejaculated the pious one, "let her fly."

"Brethren, it takes money to make a church fly," climaxed the minister.

"Amen," said the brother, "let her walk."

The price, that's the pinch. And it's not difficult to observe that whether a person succeeds or fails depends largely on whether or not he is willing to pay the price it takes.

People Suffering

It struck me as incomprehensible that I should be allowed to lead such a happy life when so many people were wrestling with care and suffering.— *Dr. Albert Schweitzer, on returning for a rest from his work as a medical missionary in Africa*

Bears in the Dark

When the son of the famous Philadelphia lawyer, George Wharton Pepper, was about four years old, his father suddenly turned on the light in his nursery to demonstrate to him that there were no bears present.

Like so many demonstrations, however, this one proved unconvincing.

"The kind of bears I see," the child said, "are the kind that only come out in the dark."

It is in the darkness of unintelligent thinking that there lurk fears and jealousies and hatreds and animosities that terrify and poison us. In the light of positive thinking, in the belief in limitless good, they have no existence. It is we ourselves who choose where we shall live—in the darkness or in the light. *Sunshine Magazine*

The Way

To every man there openeth
A Way, and Ways, and a Way.
And the High Soul climbs the High Way,
And the Low Soul gropes the Low,
And in between, on the misty flats,
The rest drift to and fro.
But to every man there openeth
A High Way, and a Low.
And every man decideth
The way his soul shall go.

John Oxenham

He Shut the Door

That versatile Australian writer, F. W. Boreham, tells us that in his congregation there was a man of unusual serenity. One Thanksgiving eve this man came bringing him a basket of freshly gathered fruit, and as they sat talking, Mr. Boreham asked him for the secret of the confidence and serenity which almost radiated from him. After some hesitation he replied, "I've always made it a rule that when I shut the door, I've shut the door."

And then he went on to explain that it used to be his habit to go to bed taking all his troubles and his fears with him. He could not sleep. His health was being undermined. One night in this condition he got up and went to the window. It was a beautiful night—"The garden below and the fields beyond were flooded in silvery moonlight. The perfect tranquility mocked the surging tumult of my brain," he said. "Why had I locked the office door so carefully if I wished all the ledgers and cash books and order forms to follow me home? Why had I closed the bedroom door so carefully if I wished all the cares of life to follow me in? I knelt down there at the windowsill, with the delicious air of the still night caressing my face, and then and there asked God to forgive me, and since then, when I've shut a door, I've shut a door." Here was a man, you see, who set the Lord, not only before him, but behind him. *Harold Cooke Phillips*

Money

Dr. Daniel A. Poling said that he learned one of the great lessons of life in a village barber shop when he was a lad.

One man of the village who had large material gains was speaking, and he said, "Money buys everything." The implications were unmistakable.

The barber, who was old and stooped and devout, shook out his frayed apron, adjusted his iron-rimmed spectacles, smiled, nodded and said, "Yes, money buys everything but three things—health, happiness and heaven."

"I was a small boy in the barber shop that day, and I have not forgotten," said Dr. Poling.

Make the Bold Choice, Think and Speak Out

To protect the precious heritage, the great gifts of principle and conviction, make the bold choice.

Follow the path of the independent thinker. Expose your ideas to the dangers of controversy.

Speak your mind and fear less the label of "crackpot" than the stigma of conformity. And on issues that seem important, stand up and be counted at any cost.

In the end, despite all the buffetings and ridicule you may have to take, intellectual courage will not destroy the American citizen.

But intellectual cowardice will. If you want a sure prescription for defeat, it is this: play it safe, stifle your thoughts, hold your tongue, flatten your intellectual profile.

If one stands up and is counted from time to time one may get knocked down.

But remember this: a man flattened by an opponent can get up again.

A man flattened by conformity stays down for good. *Thomas J. Watson, Jr.*

As You Leave

The following was found in a church bulletin and is worth copying.
AS YOU LEAVE CHURCH, may God grant you:
Enough darkness—to see the light;
Enough trials—to evaluate rest;
Enough conviction—to seek redemption;
Enough tears—to understand love;
Enough kindness—to lift burdens;
Enough grace—to shield sinners;
Enough silence—to hear the Spirit;
Enough vision—to reflect Christ.

Lutheran Digest

Some Kind of Pulpit

Everyone occupies some kind of pulpit and preaches some sort of sermon every day.

True Nobility

There is nothing noble in being superior to some other man. True nobility is being superior to your previous self. *Hindu Proverb*

No Other Solution

In the final analysis there is no other solution to man's progress but the day's honest work, the day's honest decisions, the day's generous utterances, and the day's good deed. *Clare Boothe Luce*

194

The Commodore's Prayer

A friend once gave a copy of the following prayer to Commodore John W. Caunce, Master of the majestic Queen Elizabeth of the Cunard Fleet. The Commodore had this prayer framed in his quarters. He often showed it to passengers who visited him. Many people know the prayer; but its origin it obscure:

Lord, thou knowest better than I know myself that I am growing older and will some day be old. Keep me from the fatal habit of thinking I must say something on every subject and on every occasion. Release me from craving to straighten out everybody's affairs. Make me thoughtful but not moody, helpful but not bossy. With my vast store of wisdom, it seems a pity not to use it all, but Thou knowest, Lord, that I want a few friends at the end.

Keep my mind free from the recital of endless details; give me wings to get to the point. Seal my lips on my aches and pains. They are increasing and love of rehearsing them is becoming sweeter as the years go by. I dare not ask for grace enough to enjoy the tales of others' pains, but help me to endure them with patience.

I dare not ask for improved memory, but for a growing humility and a lessening cocksureness when my memory seems to clash with the memories of others. Teach me the glorious lesson that occasionally I may be mistaken.

Keep me reasonably sweet; I do not want to be a saint—some of them are so hard to live with—but a sour old person is one of the crowning works of the devil. Give me the ability to see good things in unexpected places and talents in unexpected people. And give me, Lord, the grace to tell them so. Amen.

The Real Measure

When God measures a man, He puts the tape around the heart instead of the head.

The Rules

A Scottish minister, asked if he thought it wrong to take a walk in the country on Sunday, said, "Well, as I see it, there's no harm in takin' a walk on the Sawbath, sae long as ye dinna enjoy yourself."

He Quit

"Why did you stop singing in the choir, Thomas?"

"Well, one Sunday I was sick and didn't sing, and a lot of people in the congregation asked if the organ had been fixed."

Conscience

Conscience may help some, but it's the fear of getting caught that keeps some of us straight.

Purpose

If Heaven creates a man, there must be some use for him. *Chinese Proverb*

For Others

What we have done for ourselves alone, dies with us; what we have done for others and the world, remains and is immortal. *Albert Pike*

General Washington's Order

In an order issued by General George Washington in New York in July 1775, appeared the following precept, which is rarely practiced in the present day:

"The General is sorry to be informed that the foolish and wicked practice of profane cursing and swearing, a vice heretofore little known in an American army, is growing into fashion. He hopes the officers will, by example as well as by influence, endeavor to check it, and that both they and the men will reflect that we can have little hope of the blessing of Heaven on our arms if we insult it by our impiety and folly. Added to this it is a vice so mean and low, without any temptation, that every man of sense and character detests and despises it."

Lee's Advice

Long after Appomattox, General Robert E. Lee attended the christening of a friend's child. The mother asked the General if he could give her a few words of advice to pass on to her son when he grew old enough to appreciate them. Thinking back over his own life of suffering and struggle, General Lee said, "Teach him to deny himself."

Building the Temple of God

The Jews have a beautiful legend about the building of the Temple. On the Temple site two brothers had adjoining farms. One brother was married and had children; the other brother had no wife or children. When the harvest time came around, the brother who was married and had children said to himself, "My brother over yonder has no wife or children, and lives a lonely life. I will cheer his heart by taking some of my sheaves and adding to his harvest." And so he did. But the other brother said to himself, "My brother over yonder has a wife and many children and many cares. I will help him by taking of my sheaves and adding to his harvest." Thus, it was that each morning each brother's stack of sheaves rose higher, and both brothers wondered how it happened. At length the mystery was solved. One night as the harvest moon was shining, the two brothers met one another, each with his arms full of sheaves and bound for his brother's field. There where they met one another that night, according to the legend, rose the temple of God. *Clarence Edward Macartney*

The Biggest Shovel

A famous philanthropist was once asked, "How are you able to give so much, and still have so much?"

"Well," replied the generous man, "as I shovel out, He shovels in; and the Lord has a bigger shovel than I have."

Prayer

Prayer is one of life's greatest privileges. It is not a kind of magic talisman, as some earnest souls seem to regard it, but a way by which we can lay hold upon spiritual power. It unites God's limitless power with frail human effort. *William T. McElroy*

For Great Purposes

I have never doubted that God created man for great purposes nor that man has the potentiality within himself to achieve God's goal for him. *Preston Bradley*

Images

Remember the story of the sculptor Pygmalion who made a marble statue so beautiful everyone envied it? So perfect was it he fell in love with it, hung it with flowers and jewels, spent day after day in rapt admiration of it, believed in it, until presently his higher self poured its vital force into that image and gave it the breath of life.

There is more than pagan mythology to that story. There is this truth in it—any man can set before his mind's eye the image of the figure he himself would like to be, and then breathe the breath of life into it merely by keeping that image before his subconscious mind as the model on which to do its daily building. *Robert Collier, Good Business*

Do Something More

It is not enough merely to exist. It's not enough to say, "I'm earning enough to live and to support my family. I do my work well. I'm a good father. I'm a good husband. I'm a good churchgoer." That's all very well. But you must do something more. Seek always to do some good, somewhere. Every man has to seek in his own way to make his own self more noble and to realize his own true worth. You must give some time to your fellowman. *Albert Schweitzer*

An Opportunity Almost Lost

I would like, in closing, to remind you that you do not know the power of God in your life, personally, unless you will prepare the way for him to come in. Those valleys that have been areas of compromise need to be exalted. Those hills of pride and aggression need to be made low. Those crooked places where we have been guilty of self-seeking and self-manipulation for the sake of using others, they need to be straightened out. The rough places where we have been guilty of the things that have built barriers and problems between us and other people need to be made plain. But the only way this will become true in your life and mine is to let God be God. Let God come in and be Master in our experience.

Years ago the great musician, composer, performer, Mendelssohn, was on a vacation in Germany and went out to a little village. There was an old church in that village, and in that church an old organ. And so he went down to the church, wanting to see if it was open and whether he could go in and play a bit at the organ. And as he came up to the church and opened the door and stepped inside he heard the strains of music. He sat down in the back pew and listened as the old organist was there practicing. After some time he slipped out of the bench and went up to the organist and reached out and put his hand on his shoulder and said, "Pardon me, but would you let me play for just a few minutes." The old organist looked at him and gave him a sharp reply that said, in essence, "No, this is my organ. I play. It's not for any one else." Mendelssohn stood there and listened a few moments. A little later he put out his hand and said, "Please, just for a few minutes. I won't hurt the organ." And again the old organist gave him a rebut. And after a few minutes, Mendelssohn again put his hand on the organist's shoulder and said, "Just five minutes—I won't hurt the instrument—just five minutes." And the old organist slid off the bench and Mendolssohn seated himself at the console of the organ and began to play. Five minutes, ten minutes, fifteen—twenty—half an hour—forty-five minutes, and the old organist was standing there, with tears running down his cheeks, listening. Suddenly Mendelssohn stopped, and looked up, embarrassed that he had played so long. The old organist leaned forward and said, "Who are you?" And he looked up and simply said, "Why, I'm Mendelssohn." The old organist threw his hands up in the air and said, "Alas, I almost lost the opportunity to have the master play my organ."

It would be a tragedy at the end of your life or mine if we had to say, "I lost the opportunity to have the Master play my organ." Let God be God in your life. That's the job of the present, and the meaning of success for today and tomorrow. *Myron R. Augsburger*

What He Wanted

I've been having fun this Christmas season, but it has been with a purpose. I've been asking a lot of people a question which is not a superficial one. I've been asking them to tell me what they wanted for Christmas. And I've noted something. It's much more difficult to answer that question the older you get. A child answers quickly, a bicycle, a train set! There are many fathers known to buy their children a train set long before the children can even run them. But a child will want a play track set with cars.

As they get a little older, as a teenager, they may want a car itself. But as we get older it's more and more difficult for us to put into words what we really want for Christmas. Perhaps the clue to that comes out in David Garroway. Some of you will remember him as one of the first television personalities—he began the TODAY show. After he had become quite well-to-do, David Garroway was asked one day about his sense of Christmas, he said, "I've noticed that when people are asked what they want for Christmas, nine times out of ten they answer with something material." He said, "That used to be amusing to me, but it's not amusing to me any longer. I happen to be," he said, "one of those people who can afford anything he wants, but I find what I really want, I can't buy at all. I want peace. Peace of mind. Peace of soul. The kind of peace you have when you don't really want any thing."

As we get older we begin to sort things out, and as I've asked that plaguing question I have found that I'm getting quite different answers from people. I've usually prefaced it, with a child by saying: what if you had everything you wanted, or, you had all the money in the world and you could buy anything you wanted, then what would you like? One little child threw me a curve, he said, "I'd like happiness," and then he added, "for others." How tender. It's like the little girl who prayed at the end of the day, "God, I had a great time today," and then she added, "I hope you've had a good time, too." *Ernest J. Lewis*

Index

Propriety, 61
Prosperity, 118, 157, 186
Protoplasm, 120
Proverbs: Arab, 182; Chinese,
 23, 70, 83, 92, 104, 115, 131,
 134, 164, 182, 183, 196; Greek,
 182; Hebrew, 182; Hindu, 194;
 Persian, 117, 182; Swedish,
 130, 131, 134, 135; Turkish, 182
Prunes, 56
Psychiatrist, 101, 158, 177
Psychoanalyst, 58
Psychology, 89
Psychotic, 58
Ptolemy, 110
Public, 79; debt, 161; office, 155,
 187; speaking 13–17, 143
Puddle, 90
Pullover, 142
Pulpit, 194
Pumpernickel, 159
Punctuality, 79, 91, 133
Punctuation, 91
Puppy, 119, 178
Purpose of life, 51
Pusey, Nathan, 110
Push-button finger, 79
Pygmalion, 197
Pyramids, 190
Pythagoras, 115

Quality merchandise, 65
Quarrels, 143
Quartet, 170
Question-and-answer periods,
 33, 62
Quillen, Robert, 184
Quoting oneself, 77

Rabbi, 31, 45
Rabbit, 177
Race, 181, 184; horse, 122;
 track, 64, 100
Radical, 76, 157
Radio, 172

Raffle tickets, 64
Railroad: construction, 97;
 crossing, 55
Railroads, 23, 32
Raise, 45, 91
Rambling wreck from Georgia
 Tech, 135
Ram, hyraulic, 67
Randall, Henry S., 163
Raphael, 88, 152
Rascoe, Burton, 76
"The Raven," 151
Reading, 120
Reality, shadow of, 117
Recall, things you can't, 117
Recessions, 23
Records, 22
Red Cross, 167
Red lights, 59
Reform and reformers, 24, 118,
 131, 144, 160
Regan, Gerald A., 55
Rehabilitation, 140
Relatives, 53, 176
Relativity, 73, 148
Religion, 37–48, 72, 102, 192–
 199
Remarque, Erich Maria, 105
Rembrandt, H. van Rijn, 150
Remington, Frederic, 153
Remote control, 89
Repairmen: garage, 125;
 telephone, 58
Repartee, 72
Report card, 105, 107
Republicans, 130
Reputation, 76
Research, 102
Resources, natural, 160
Rest, 58, 77, 89
Restaurants, 56
Restlessness, 185
Retirement, 84, 91
Reviews of plays, 71
Revolution, 157
Rewarding labor, 94
Rich: getting, 73; the, 131

About the Author

Author and editor of over 40 books, many of them selections for public speakers and toastmasters, Herbert V. Prochnow has had an illustrious career in both the public and private sectors. He took his Ph.D. at Northwestern University, and he also holds honorary doctoral degrees from seven other colleges and universities. He was the President and Director of the First National Bank of Chicago, President of the Chicago Association of Commerce and Industry and he even wrote a financial column for several years for the *Chicago Sunday Tribune*. He served as Deputy Under Secretary of State, Alternate Governor for the U.S. of the International Bank and International Monetary Fund, and Secretary of the Federal Advisory Council of the Federal Reserve System. He lives in Evanston, Illinois.